C000084772

The Quest to Regain Paradise

The Quest to Regain Paradise

Richard Hewitt

**WHITE RABBIT
PROCLAMATIONS**

Copyright © 2013 by Richard Hewitt

Published by White Rabbit Proclamations

The moral right of Richard Hewitt to be identified as the author of this work has been asserted in accordance with the Copyright, Designs and Patents Act, 1988.

All rights reserved. No part of this publication may be reproduced or transmitted in any form or by any means, electronic or mechanical, including photocopy, recording, or any information storage and retrieval system, without permission in writing from the author.

A CIP catalogue reference for this book is available from the British Library.

ISBN 978-0-9576060-0-5 (Paperback)
ISBN 978-0-9576060-1-2 (epub)
ISBN 978-0-9576060-2-9 (mobi)

Cover design by White Rabbit Proclamations

Prepared and printed by:

York Publishing Services Ltd
64 Hallfield Road
Layerthorpe
York YO31 7ZQ

Tel: 01904 431213

Website: www.yps-publishing.co.uk

Bringing the esoteric

revelation to the masses

About the author

Richard Hewitt is a teacher from Yorkshire. After gaining the prestigious Fringe First Award for his part in a devised production at the Edinburgh Fringe Festival, he went on to gain his degree from the Department of Aeronautical and Mechanical Engineering, at Salford University. He then joined the Logistics Systems Dynamics Group in Cardiff, a world leader in its approach to seamless supply chain management, where he carried out research into reengineering hospital supply pipelines. He then moved back to Yorkshire, where he gained a post graduate certificate in teaching from the University College of Ripon and York St John.

Richard's work, *The Quest To Regain Paradise*, is an outcome of two decades of private research into the revelatory story that has been secreted and passed down through the ages in the teachings and rituals of secret organisations, fraternities and syndicates across the globe. After consulting with doctors, professors, film directors, literary agents, bestselling authors, demonic-magicians, high ranking secret society members and Grand Masters of esoteric orders, he has at last produced what can only be described as the resolution to the mysteries.

Acknowledgements

The list is almost endless, but I would like to begin by generally thanking the plethora of people in this work, named and unnamed, who have contributed to helping piece together the history of the quest to regain Paradise. Special thanks must go to the seasoned writer and all-round 'good egg', Gary Smailes, for without his editing skills and knowledge of book proposals I might never have gained a literary agent. Also, great thanks to my former literary agent, Robin Wade, who put me on the trail of the Hebrew Enigma machine that was built into the temple gateway. I hope we prove Mark wrong, Robin, but only time will tell. Most of all, my deepest thanks must go out to Lily Lane and to the Guardians who provided me with an insight into the deepest elements of the quest. All is not lost!

Thanks Dad for your take on everything and support. I hope I have done well and you are proud. And Lizzie, you are my Lily, always.

Both the publisher and I have not added material to this work that would intentionally offend, cause distress or defame. If requested by an individual or organisation mentioned in the work, we would remove material relating to them and submit an apology if appropriate in future print runs.

To the Reader:
And Was Jerusalem Builded Here?

Fact: At 17:00 BST on Tuesday, October 11, 2011, three men employed by a syndicate associated with an arcane quest to regain humankind's lost, biblical Paradise entered Holy Cross Abbey, in Co. Tipperary, and stole one of its sacred relics. Unaware of the existence of the syndicate and the importance of the relic to this quest, the BBC and *The Irish Times* reported that investigating police were simply baffled by the theft. In order to stay true to the prophesy associated with the quest, the relic would have soon after been hidden in a purpose-built temple, in Jerusalem, in preparation for an unimaginable event. Not Jerusalem in the Holy Land, but the original Jerusalem that appears surreptitiously in the great British hymn, *Jerusalem*; the Jerusalem built in England, in Ancient Eborakon, the now City of York.

It happened in 2009, on the Winter Solstice. After sacrificing two decades of my life piecing together the quest to regain Paradise, I finally located the ancient temple in York that was built to act as the gateway, the nexus, the portal between this world and the celestial realm.

I know. This all sounds like the beginning to a religious-occult, Hollywood adventure movie or some such like. But if I have discovered the gateway to Paradise, the implications are perhaps as far reaching as discovering God Himself. It will change everything.

From what I have witnessed, I have to conclude that the quest to regain Paradise was designed and given to us by a higher force, secreted, hidden within our psyche, within our very DNA; its exquisite content translated by a chosen few over the ages and secretly preserved in scripture, mystery systems and in the intimate nature of mysterious characters that appear in cultures across the globe. And then there is the prophesised end time, when a group of adepts will take possession of the divine secrets and sacred relics required for the final celestial battle; the battle of all history, for all history, the battle to regain our Paradise.

The following chronicle is based solely on real life events. It will not only guide you to the temple gateway, but also reveal the pathway to Paradise itself.

RH, Eborakon, Winter Solstice, 2012.

1ˢᵗ Degree

Follow the White Rabbit

Way back in 1989, as part of an enthusiastic group of young people, I helped devise a theatrical play around a forty foot high climbing wall for the Edinburgh Fringe Festival, entitled *E56B*. In our second week of performing we were amazed to find that we had been secretly observed and awarded the festival's highest accolade, the coveted Fringe First. As part of the prize-giving ceremony we shook hands with an array of elderly Scottish people, one of which made a strange comment that profoundly changed the direction of my life.

"I believe your play is as surreal as the White Rabbit from *Alice's Adventures in Wonderland*," the woman had whispered in my ear and then winked. It was not the nature of her words that took me by surprise, but the primeval sense of foreboding that followed. For the briefest moment a long forgotten memory was stirred. I was a small child again, lost, wandering aimlessly on a pebbled beach in Cornwall.

"The White Rabbit," I had muttered in return. "I'll have to remember that one." And I did.

When the exhilarating experience of the Fringe was over and I had returned home to Yorkshire things seemed different, almost like a spell had been cast. The woman's words began to feature in a reoccurring dream, where the White Rabbit was dancing intermittently on a crescent moon to the cacophony of an insane orchestra. He then beckoned me to follow him into his warren, which held a peculiar aroma of incense and roots that shone like stars. Each night, as I clambered towards the disc of light that formed the exit to the warren, I awoke to find myself searching for air.

The White Rabbit

In the years following my Fringe adventure, I became obsessed with the White Rabbit, and in an attempt to somehow make sense of my troubling encounter with him, I spent much time researching his mysterious character.

While collecting examples of his use in the Western world, I discovered that he was often depicted alongside the crescent moon, just like in my dream. You will have probably noticed this odd partnership when looking at christening and Easter cards. I also found him alongside the crescent moon on ancient artefacts, the essence of which still appears in ornamentation from the Far East (Fig. 1, left). However, it was in the recesses of Mesoamerican mythology where I discovered the true astronomical nature of the White Rabbit; it symbolised the white-planet Venus, alongside the crescent moon, as the eternal mother of the sky.[1]

Figure 1

Even though I was unaware of its significance at the time, I found it telling that the symbol of Islam incorporated an unadulterated version of this ancient astronomical partnership (fig. 1, right), which was shown to the prophet Mohammed as part of his initial Vahy or revelation from Allah.[2]

But what caught my imagination at the time was that the White Rabbit had been used throughout the ages to represent various secrets, such as the one held by a 17th century secret society called the Rosicrucian or Rosy Cross Order. Here the Rosicrucians used the White Rabbit as a metaphor to represent their search for a secret, as illustrated in the strange drawing (fig. 2) by the 17th century Rosicrucian-alchemist, Basilius Valentinus.[3] As you can see, the Rosicrucian adepts are destined to follow the White Rabbit, since he will undoubtedly disappear down the hole with their secret.

Figure 2

While attempting to unravel the nature of this Rosicrucian secret, I discovered that the well-known phrase "follow the White Rabbit" did not appear in *Alice's Adventures in Wonderland*. This triggered a number of questions: Why and how had this mysterious phrase become rendered into the human psyche? Did it perhaps arc back to the Rosicrucian secret? Moreover, is this why the White Rabbit had been used as a mysterious beckoning-icon not only by Lewis Carroll, but also in an early episode of Star Trek, *The Matrix* film, and in strange songs that impart a sense of mystery, such as Jefferson Aeroplane's *White Rabbit*?

You Couldn't Make it Up

My research eventually hit a dead end and with these questions left unanswered I returned to my daily life. It was not until just after the start of the new millennium, years later, that my interest in the White Rabbit was reignited.

To my delight, I was given the opportunity to follow in the footsteps of the Rosicrucians, to physically follow the White Rabbit. I was told about this seemingly impossible concept by a very knowledgeable man called George Child, who for many years has resided at the Old Vicarage Bookshop in Wakefield. George is a colourful yet seasoned character, who is seen by many as a modern-sage of the darker mysteries. If you ever decide to visit him, be sure to ask about his appearance in a newspaper article that delves into some of his intriguing adventures. Be warned though, his meticulous use of strange facts and seemingly unrelated global events could set you on a train of thought that is, well, simply too scary to ignore.

On the morning in question, during my visit to his bookshop, George and I were talking about the appearance of stone-carved demonic beasts in medieval churches. An odd subject I agree, but in combination with a previous conversation about Gothic architecture, it acted as the catalyst for his provocative fable about Lewis Carroll's stone-carved White Rabbit, which resides in a medieval church.

To begin the tale George turned over his miniature, Calumet-style smoking pipe and moved it up into the corner of his mouth.

"A long time ago I had a certain affiliation with the Rosicrucian-Masonic lodge in Sheffield, the Royal Arch Chapter of Paradise, Lodge No. 139.[4] The Master of the lodge told me a fable that explained why Lewis Carroll used the White Rabbit in his story. It's not at first obvious, but Carroll's story is surreal because it is full of Rosicrucian symbolism."

George waited for a response, but I said nothing.

"It was when Carroll moved to Yorkshire, as a small boy, as part of his home tuition, that his clergyman-father took him to the surrounding churches to explain about the strange symbolism left behind by the medieval carpenters and stonemasons. This is how he came to know about the stone-carved White Rabbit and its importance to the Rosicrucian Order. This is why he later used the icon in his story. He used it to keep the Rosicrucian secret alive."[5]

"So this is why the Rosicrucian adepts were trying to catch the White Rabbit. I found a picture of this, years ago. So tell me, what's the secret then George?"

"Well, just as I was told, a clue to the nature of their secret can be found with the church's stone White Rabbit."

"So where's the church then? Do you know?"

"Of course, but I have to explain something first. If you do decide to follow the White Rabbit, the trail will undoubtedly go cold at Ripon, I know, I've been there. To get to Ripon though, you will first have to visit St. Mary's, where the White Rabbit resides, which can be found in Beverley, within the old Diocese of York."

Having recently moved to York, I explained that I could easily make the trip to Beverley in under an hour. I then thanked George for the intriguing opportunity and headed back home to prepare for my surreal journey to follow the White Rabbit.

The next morning, after a short tour of Beverley, I eventually found St. Mary's Church, but for some reason felt obliged to hang around in the porch until the morning service was over. As the worshipers began to leave, I grabbed the opportunity to slip inside. As the vicar finished shaking the last hand I moved in swiftly and introduced myself.

"I know it might sound a little strange vicar, but I am on a mission to follow the White Rabbit."

He laughed, clapped his hands together and without a word guided me over to the icon in question (fig. 3).

Figure 3

After reciting George's strange fable to the vicar, he shrugged his shoulders.

"Like I told all the others, I must be honest I know nothing of a Rosicrucian secret, only that this stone rabbit was probably the main inspiration for Lewis Carroll's White Rabbit. I believe Ripon Cathedral in North Yorkshire also has a legitimate claim for Carroll's inspiration. You will find their White Rabbit upon the Cathedral's famous misericords."

"Yes, I sort of know about the Ripon connection. Misericords?"

"Yes, misericords. If you look in the wooden stalls at Ripon Cathedral you will find them, and the White Rabbit. I believe Beverley Minster, just up the road, has a fine set of misericords. I would certainly recommend a visit."

Mysterious Misericords

Before rushing off to Ripon, I decided to look into these so-called misericords and without too much trouble found that they were tiny seats for monks to rest on, while taking part in long religious services. As you can see (fig. 4), the undersides of these seats hold strange scenes that were carved-out by the medieval artisans.

Figure 4

Unfortunately, no one had done any detailed research into the nature of these strange carvings, but some commentators suggested that they had Pagan origins, and that many of them were destroyed over the ages because they were seen as "improper".[6] However, while taking pictures of the misericords in Beverley Minster, I was told a romantic theory by an elderly gentleman called Stan

Byatt, which explained just why the medieval artisans had carved the strange scenes. Stan was not only a veteran member of Beverley's Masonic lodge, but also a guide at the Minster.

"The 12th century artisans, metal, stone and wood workers, were part of a fraternal network of mystery-craft lodges," Stan explained to me. "As part of their craft teachings, they were given access to the content of a story of immense importance, a story that is now lost to time."

"Lost to time?" I asked.

"Yes, the extent of this story is still hidden within the misericord carvings."

He stretched out and tapped a misericord with his brass-tipped walking stick (fig. 5).

"What I do know is that this particular scene depicts a special moment from the story, where an anonymous adept is fighting with a griffin for a treasure; a secret treasure that is lost, but at the same time has to be found."

Figure 5

"What sort of treasure?"

"Ah, no one can be told what it is. Like my father told me, only the eternal Fool goes in search of this particular treasure."

This romantic idea of a lost treasure was dancing in my mind when I eventually made the scenic drive to Ripon, in search of the Cathedral's White Rabbit. Once inside the Cathedral I visited the souvenir shop and found a pamphlet that explained all about its Lewis Carroll connection. However, I needed more help and hoping for some insight I struck-up a conversation with the woman running the shop.

"I'm following the White Rabbit. The vicar from St. Mary's in Beverley pointed me in your direction."

"Oh, this sounds like an excellent adventure. I'll shut the shop and take you to see our poor little creature."

"Poor little creature?"

She shooed me out of the shop, locked the door and headed off towards the heart of the Cathedral. Without delay I followed in her footsteps, until she stopped and pointed with a smile at the misericord containing Carroll's White Rabbit (fig. 6). As I inspected the content of the scene my heart began to race because it again depicted the fearsome griffin. Here it was not fighting with the warrior, but attacking the White Rabbit.

Figure 6

As I left the Cathedral, I realised that George was right; the trail had quite literally gone cold at Ripon.

Nevertheless, I wanted to know more. When I visited George to tell him about my White Rabbit adventure, he listened intently and then began questioning me.

"Didn't the vicar at Beverley tell you about the misericords?" He asked.

"Yes, you know he did. That's why I went to Beverley Minster and then to Ripon."

George laughed.

"Ah, the vicar sold you a mock turtle, a mock turtle indeed. He did not want you rooting around. You need to search through wonderland."

"What do you mean mock turtle? Do I need to read through Carroll's story?"

"Look, if you truly want to follow the White Rabbit, you will have to go back to St. Mary's in Beverley."

"This all sounds a little sketchy George, at least give me a clue."

"OK. What I can tell you is that the White Rabbit was employed by the medieval artisans, Rosicrucians and ultimately by Lewis Carroll because of its esoteric meaning. It is the symbol for an age-old *quest* to reacquire a treasure that was taken from the human race."

"A treasure, Stan mentioned this. But what treasure could have possibly been taken from the human race?"

He placed his finger on my temple and tapped three times.

"The treasure that many believe God took from us, Paradise young man, Paradise."

"So you're saying there's a quest to regain Paradise?"

"Is Paradise something that should not be sought? Just be sure to make the trip back to St. Mary's."

Sufficiently intrigued by George's proposition, I made my way back to St. Mary's, which on this occasion was empty, apart from a solitary sparrow dancing up and down in the rafters. Unsure of what I was supposed to be looking for, I started by scanning the architecture for other examples of the White Rabbit. In doing this I discovered that St. Mary's had its own set of misericords, accompanied by a sign explaining, "These seats must not be handled". Hesitantly, but at the same time undeterred by the sign, I began lifting the seats to examine their strange carvings. Each creak of the medieval oak caused me to wince, then bob up-and-down to check that the coast was clear. In fear of being caught I quickly photographed the carvings and then cautiously made my way out of the church.

On my return home, I switched on my computer and set about downloading all the photographs, and soon came across a misericord scene that again took me aback. It held two rabbits and two griffins clawing at a small tree (fig.7).

Figure 7

After several minutes studying the scene, I realised that the griffins were striking a common pose. I say common, because in heraldry the all important shield, which holds the symbols of its owner's provenance, is usually protected or supported by mythical creatures, like griffins or dragons (fig. 8). So were the griffins there to protect something, as part of the artisans' lost story? But without any real insight into the story, I knew that I was just clutching at straws.

Figure 8

As Clear As Soup

Thinking back to my last conversation with George, and not having read *Wonderland* for several years, I settled down with a bottle of wine and began the trip down memory lane. I knew that George always chose his words wisely, and I was not surprised to find that one of the chapters was entitled *The Mock Turtle's Story*. Sure enough, half way through the chapter, I came to the episode where Alice meets a griffin. As I read on, I found nothing of value in the text, other than it gave even more weight to the idea that the misericord scenes had inspired Carroll to write his story. But what really drew Carroll to these scenes? Did they just catch his eye, or was there in fact a deeper, more profound reason for his motivation?

On the following Saturday morning I posed these questions to George, and for some reason he seemed to get a little irate.

"I have already told you, Reverend Charles Lutwidge Dodgson [Lewis Carroll] had been well aware of the esoteric significance of the misericord scenes; they are linked to the artisans' lost story and the Rosicrucian secret, as part of the quest to regain Paradise."

"But if Carroll knew about this secret quest, why would he want to give it up to all and sundry George?"

He turned over his pipe.

"Carroll did not give up the secret. Like the others before him, he just preserved it for a very specific generation to find."

Solomon's House – The College of the Six Dayes Workes

I spent several weeks searching for information about the Rosicrucians' involvement with a quest to regain Paradise, but found nothing of real significance. So in a radical move I made contact with a modern version of the Rosicrucian Order, the Ancient Mystical Order Rosae Crucis (AMORC). I wrote a letter to its American-based Grand Master or Imperator, using an address from one of their old publications, the *Rosicrucian Digest*. To be honest, I did not expect a reply, since I knew that the Grand Master would be unlikely to share the Order's secrets with a woodwork teacher from York.

Sir Francis Bacon and King Solomon's House

On the morning I bent down to pick up the letter containing the AMORC acronym, I had forgotten all about my bold enquiry to the Grand Master. What struck me as odd was the signature at the bottom that read, "Thomas Anderson, Adept of the 9th Temple Degree".

Thomas began his letter by explaining that he could not divulge any of the Order's secrets to a non-member, but that he would be more than happy to help with my search for enlightenment. In an attempt to do this, he enclosed a copy of the title page and a battered introduction to the epic work called *New Atlantis*, which had been written by the 17th century Rosicrucian Grand Master, Sir Francis Bacon (Fig. 9).[1]

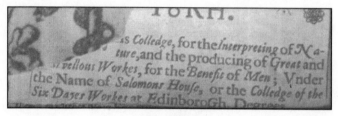

Figure 9

Thomas was also good enough to provide a little background information to help explain Bacon's inspiration for this enigmatic introduction, which I found complex, but at the same time familiar:[2]

Francis Bacon's inner-circle of Rosicrucian adepts (Salomon's House or the College of the Six Dayes Workes) had known about the existence of God's secret knowledge on earth, which is hidden within the fundamental building blocks of nature. As explained in Bacon's introduction, they were attempting to decode and acquire it for the benefit of all men, in an attempt to gain salvation for the human race. The Rosicrucian college was named Salomon's House, College of the Six Dayes Workes in tribute to the legendary Israelite king, King Salomon [modern spelling 'Solomon'], who had been entrusted with God's secret knowledge on earth. God instructed Solomon to render this knowledge into the architecture of his miraculous temple, Solomon's

Temple. He also rendered a magic key into the temple, in the form of a secret word, which could be used to unlock the divine knowledge. It was this key or word that the 17th century Rosicrucian Order had been searching for.

Captivated by this complex but absorbing idea, I set about looking into the life of King Solomon and soon found that just like Bruce, from the film *Bruce Almighty*, Solomon had used God's secret knowledge to perform many miraculous deeds. According to folklore and Jewish tradition he had the ability to control nature, talk to the animals, and he even used his God-given knowledge to enslave the netherworld demonic-Genii to help construct his 'magic' temple.[3]

According to a work produced by the famous Jewish historian, Flavius Josephus, around AD 37:

> ...the sagacity and wisdom which God had bestowed on Solomon was so great, that he exceeded the ancients who are said to have been beyond all men in understanding[4].

I also discovered that the so-called demonic-magicians, from the 15th century, were caught up with the mystery surrounding the search for Solomon's magic Key. For instance, one of their manuscripts, the *Key of Solomon*, is devoted entirely to the nature of the Key. To this end, King Solomon himself explains:

> Like as a key opens a treasure-house, so this Key alone may open the knowledge and understanding of magical arts and sciences.[5]

In an attempt to explore this idea further, I decided to go to the top and made contact with a biochemistry professor from Hull University called Edwin A. Dawes, who was not only the Honorary Vice-President of The Magic Circle in London, but also a member of the Hall of Fame of the Society of American Magicians. Unfortunately the professor's field of expertise did not cover this obscure aspect of magic, but as part of our conversation he gave me the contact details of a lady from Dalton, who passed me on to another lady who kindly invited me to the 2002 Magic Circle's Awards Banquet.

"Yes, I will post you a ticket today," the lady explained. "If you attend the banquet, you will undoubtedly come across someone with information pertaining to the age old search for the keyword that Solomon rendered into his temple. I have no doubt."

Solomon's Magic White Rabbit

On the day of the magic banquet I arrived in good time and was a little surprised to see Rolf Harris standing at the entrance to the venue.

"Are you here for the banquet?" I asked.

"Yes, I have to make a speech."

After Rolf had explained about the magic he had performed on children's television when he first came to Britain, I made my way inside and headed straight for the bar.

I found myself standing next to a group of elderly magicians, and after a few slurps of Dutch courage I waited for a lull in their boisterous conversation and casually introduced myself, explaining how I had gained my invitation to the banquet.

"I think you need to speak with my knowledgeable friend who has come all the way from Israel to be with us today," one of the magicians proposed.

He then broke from the pack and led me over to the woman in question, who was sitting alone with her back to the crowd. As he whispered in her ear for a long moment, she turned to examine my demeanour. She then offered me a seat without introduction.

"Yes, I know of the keyword associated with Solomon's magic Grimorie, the *Key of Solomon*," she explained as I settled myself into the seat. "Why do you seek it?"

"Grimoire?" I asked.

"All I can tell you is that the Rosicrucian search for the keyword is usually represented as an icon that most people would unwittingly disregard."

"What sort of icon?"

"The icon that symbolises all magic, which is eternally pulled from the magician's top hat, the plain old white rabbit."

Immediately the back of my head started to tingle, and a series of familiar images began to reel across my mind's eye, as if they were part of some old film strip. As the cognitive-cinematic experience subsided to a single flicker, I was left with an image of a still-frame, which contained the Rosicrucian adepts in pursuit of their secret; the White Rabbit, or perhaps the icon for Solomon's keyword.

Figure 2

18

What followed was a strange lecture on the pitfalls of attempting to raise demonic-spirits. I explained to the woman that I had no intention of raising any demons, especially those of my own. I then thanked her for her time and turned to make my way back to the bar. Before I could pace out a step, she took hold of my arm and proceeded to do something odd. She pulled my hand towards her face and pretended to spit in it. Shocked by this action, I tried to pull free without making a scene, but she grabbed on tight. After a few more uncomfortable moments she raised her head and looked me in the eye.

"Thank you."

"That's alright," I grumbled.

She set me free and I made my way back to the bar. When I explained to her magician-friend what had just happened, he sniggered.

"I apologise. Look, you should join our table; I'll bring up the topic of Solomon's Key at an opportune moment."

Mid-way through the meal the magician did bring up the topic of Solomon's Key, which immediately provoked an elderly magician with an array of medals attached to his jacket breast.

"The Key is not a suitable topic for this table. It's just hocus-pocus anyway."

As he was saying this he looked at me and winked.

The night progressed and towards the end of the banquet I took-up one of the empty seats next to the old magician and began bombarding him with questions.

"So can you tell me anything about Solomon's House or the College of the Six Dayes Workes from *New Atlantis*? Was this Rosicrucian college searching for Solomon's secret keyword, the White Rabbit, to unlock God's secret knowledge to gain salvation for the human race? Does all this relate to a quest to regain Paradise?"

He seemed a little bemused by my questions, but after a deep drag on his hefty cigar the stout, bald-headed magician, with beads of sweat strewn across his face, shuffled round and leaned in close.

"The extent of the powerful magic surrounding Solomon's Key has no place within the current Magic Circle, but elements of it are still used today by the Roman Catholic Church to expel demons; you know, exorcism. But to answer your questions, Solomon's House or the College of the Six Dayes Workes was a Rosicrucian version of the inner-circle of magi priests that once resided in Solomon's Temple. And yes, I do believe they had one goal in life; to acquire the keyword from Solomon's Temple, to save the human race."

"So what have the demons got to do with all this?"

"Sorry, I thought you knew that the demonic-Genii were used by Solomon to build the temple."

"Yes I did know. So did they have something to do with hiding the keyword in the temple's architecture?"

He smiled, took hold of my arm, and as part of a magic trick made a card flip over into my hand.

"Here are the details of a magic-doctor. She resides at the University of Bern in Switzerland. I am sure she will be able to open your mind."

Magic Moments

Like most people do, I initially thought that magic was based on the act of performing seemingly supernatural feats, using purely natural means. However, after contacting the Swiss magic-doctor, she proposed something a little different in one of her emails:

> Modern magic is undoubtedly a corruption of the original, which made use of demonic powers. Just like King Solomon, the early magicians supposedly conjured-up and even exorcised demons from unwitting souls. They took control of these demons using a magic circle and then instructed them to perform supernatural deeds. This is why the term Magic Circle was adopted by the modern order of magicians.

She even attached an example of what she called Solomon's Grand Magic Circle to her email, which had been used by the 15th century magicians (Fig. 10).[6]

Having looked into this issue in some depth, I found that in Arabic folklore and stories from the East, such as *One Thousand and One Knights* or *Arabian Nights*, there are many references to Solomon's demonic-magic

Figure 10

antics. To add to this, in AD 1945 a set of ancient religious 'Gnostic-magic' texts were unearthed in Egypt, which similarly talk about Solomon's involvement with demons.[7] These so-called Nag Hammadi texts (named after the place they were found) contain two-thousand year old magic stories which, according to the magic-doctor, were purposefully omitted from the Bible when it was first put together in 325 by the Roman Emperor, Constantine. As part of one of these stories called *On the Origins of the World*[8] there is an obscure reference to a demonic book that was written by King Solomon:

> Out of the entity called Death came forty-nine demons. The names and effects of the demons can be found in the *Book of Solomon*.[9]

Unfortunately the *Book of Solomon* has since been lost to time. However, according to the magic-doctor:

> Copies of the *Book of Solomon*, along with many other now missing Gnostic works, were smuggled out of Egypt and the Holy Land, in 2nd century; of course some were buried by the Gnostic sects when fleeing from the Roman authorities, like the ones found next to the Dead Sea. Many of these free-thinkers eventually found refuge in Old Occitan, southern France. Their works, which included the *Book of Solomon*, were then preserved over the ages by a series of fraternities. The *Book of Solomon* eventually resurfaced in the 15th century with the European demonic-magicians, under a more appropriate title, the *Lost Testament of Solomon* or the *Testament of Solomon* for short.

Intrigued by this theory, I took the time to secure a copy of the 15th century *Testament of Solomon*, to see if its content was at all similar to the ancient Egyptian *Book of Solomon*, which according to the quote from *On the Origins of the World* held the names and effects of Solomon's demons. It took around a month to find a copy, but it was well worth while, since I not only found a full description of the names and effects of Solomon's demons, but also a detailed description of how he used them to build his 'magic' temple containing the keyword.[10]

With this new information to hand I headed out for the bookshop, to see if George could help develop my intriguing line of enquiry.

"You are now party to an important part of the mystery," he began. "You now know that the 2nd century Gnostics, 12th century artisans, 15th century demonic-magicians and the 17th century Rosicrucians were all caught-up with Solomon and his temple for one reason..."

"Yes, they wanted to acquire the keyword to gain salvation for the human race."

"That's right. They knew that the only way to regain Paradise was by unlocking God's secret knowledge using the White Rabbit, the keyword, which was secreted within the temple's architecture. This is why the temple has appeared at the heart of most secret society teachings throughout the ages."

The Master Plan

It was late in 2002, after exhausting several lines of enquiry, that I found myself in the car listening to a radio interview featuring the Evangelical Christian, Sir Peter Vardy. I was interested in the interview for two reasons. Firstly because my brother-in-law, Darren Hewitt-Craft, was a prestige car-buyer for Vardy's firm; and secondly because, as a teacher, I was fascinated with Sir Peter's controversial involvement with the education sector.

The interviewer began by explaining all about the new and 'innovative' schools that Sir Peter had founded. He went on to say that a group of eight bishops and nine leading scientists had accused Sir Peter of allowing Creationism to be taught in the classroom.[1] The interviewer then asked what he thought about the allegations, to which he responded adamantly.

"I do not believe that the universe was created in six days."

On the Origins of the World

Fascinated by the idea of Creationism, I opened my copy of the Bible and turned to *Genesis*. After reading all about God's 'six days work' and thinking about Solomon's

House or College of the Six Dayes Workes, I found myself reading the episode that deals with the realm of Paradise. Working my way through the episode in hope of finding a reference to or even hint of a quest to regain Paradise, it soon became apparent that God had placed Adam and Eve in Paradise with two trees: a tree that would feed them forever (Tree of Life), and a tree that, ironically, held God's secret knowledge (Tree of Knowledge). I also found that God was more than happy for Adam and Eve to eat from the Tree of Life, but had specifically warned them not to eat from the Tree of Knowledge, since they would die.

This seemingly trivial investigation raised a number of questions about the Paradise story. I could not understand why God had allowed the infamous serpent-beast to coax Eve into eating from the Tree of Knowledge. While at the same time, I really wanted to know who the serpent-beast was and where he had come from. Struggling with these questions, I gave George a ring.

"Yes, I have just the thing for you," he explained. "I am a little busy at the moment, but if you call by later this afternoon I'll root it out. You're on the right track; the Beast holds a secret that is paramount to the quest to regain Paradise. He was the Instructor."

"Instructor?"

"That's right. As part of a master plan he instigated the mutiny in Paradise."

When I arrived at the shop later that day it was closed. Luckily this was not an issue, since I knew to look under the wheelie bin, where George had left things before. Moving the bin to one side, I noticed a large envelope with my name on it, which I quickly picked up and opened. When the contents slipped out onto my hand, I saw that it was a copy of the Gnostic story from Egypt, which the Swiss magic-doctor had talked about in her emails, *On the Origins of the World*; the story holding the reference to the *Book of Solomon* that held information about the names and effects of the demons that built Solomon's Temple.

From Creation to the *Book of Solomon*

After reading the first page, it was obvious that the Gnostic story held a mysterious version of the *Genesis* creation story. Here the celestial being in overall control was described as the Immortal Man of Light, and he existed in a realm made of light called Barbelo with his goddesses, Faith and Wisdom. As I turned over the page, I came to what looked like a scan of an ancient parchment, which had been translated by hand, with the title, *The Recently Discovered Gnostic Gospel of Judas*. Several parts of the parchment had been underlined and star shapes had been used to highlight one particular section.

As I looked over this section, it explained how Judas had approached Jesus to tell him that he knew where he had come from, from the realm of light, Barbelo. In response to this 'accusation', Jesus took Judas aside to explain what he described as the, "Mysteries of the Kingdom." As I turned over to the next page I noticed a hand written note:

The Immortal Man of Light had a master plan, which would one day lead to a final epic battle between the under-gods and mortals for the right to rule in Paradise...

As I continued with the story, it explained that the goddesses, Faith and Wisdom, had been instructed by the Immortal Man of Light to put this monumental master plan into action. In the first instance they formed a creative entity called Yaltabaoth, who just like God from the *Genesis* story brought forth light from the darkness and ultimately formed the earth. Yaltabaoth then gave birth to the so-called Authorities or under-gods of the celestial and terrestrial realms. One of the Authorities, an under-god called Sabaoth, was then purposefully seduced by the goddess Faith and given instructions on how to continue the master plan. In response to Sabaoth's 'disloyalty', his father, Yaltabaoth, retaliated, giving birth to the entity called Death, who in turn gave birth to the demons of the world.

It was at this point in the story that I came to the quote concerning the *Book of Solomon*. On seeing the familiar quote, I rooted out my copy of the 15th century magic version of the *Book of Solomon* (the Lost *Testament of Solomon*), to see if it held any references to Yaltabaoth, his Authorities, or even the Immortal Man of Light. Amazingly, I discovered a passage which explained that King Solomon had been given a special ring to enslave the demonic-Genii to help build his temple. I am sure that you can imagine my reaction when I read that it was the under-god Sabaoth, from the 2nd century Gnostic story, *On the Origins of the World*, who provided Solomon with the ring:

Take, O Solomon, king, son of David, the gift which the Lord God has sent thee, the highest Sabaoth.[2]

Enthralled with the appearance of the Egyptian-Gnostic under-god in the 15th century European magic story, I gave George a ring at home. I was expecting him to congratulate me on my tantalising discovery, but he passed it by as if it were old news and began talking about the 'true' nature of Solomon's Temple. More specifically, about the keyword that could be used to unlock God's secret knowledge.

"The story surrounding the building of Solomon's Temple is a red herring of sorts. The temple-story is in fact a Gnostic allegory or metaphor for the disposition of the human race, which over the years was adopted by various mystery schools, including, the medieval-religious artisans, demonic magicians, Rosicrucians and ultimately the Freemasons. Solomon's Temple is actually a Gnostic metaphor for the architecture of the living temple that holds God's secret knowledge."

"A living temple?" I asked.

"Yes, the basic teachings of these secret fraternities state that the candidate is a personification of the temple, and that the end goal is to understand just what the temple holds, God's secret knowledge, from the Tree of Knowledge."

"But what about the keyword for unlocking it? Is this in the temple, us I mean, too?"

"Yes, that's right, and one day the human race, as the metaphorical White Rabbit, will use the keyword to unlock this knowledge to fulfil the celestial master plan, to regain Paradise."

"Sorry, we are the White Rabbit?

"Look, just keep this idea in mind and you will not go far wrong."

Man, Wo-Man and the Instructor

After returning to the Gnostic story, I found that Yaltabaoth and the Authorities were also given the power to create a creature, who they modelled in their own likeness, in the form of the first human, Adam. When I cross referenced this event with the Bible, it appeared to me that God, just like Yaltabaoth, had made Adam with help from some other celestial force. For instance, in *Genesis* 1:26, God says:

> Let Us make man in Our own image, according to Our likeness...

Obviously it could be the case that God was using the word "Us" in the royal sense, but with the Gnostic story in mind, I could not help but think that the "Us" might have been a reference to a group of under-gods like the Authorities, which for some reason had been omitted from the *Genesis* story. As I read on, I also discovered that the 'first' Eve in Paradise was called Eve of Life, and that she was not Adam's partner as such, but an all-knowing entity that was sent by the Immortal Man of Light to educate him. To this end, Eve of Life explained to Adam that the Authorities wanted him to remain in Paradise, so they could observe him and gloat about their creative exploits. When the Authorities learned of Eve of Life's provocative actions they confronted her and forced her to leave. However, before her departure, she conceived two children, a boy, and a girl who she simply named Eve. It was this Eve that was placed in Paradise with Adam as his partner, while her brother was given knowledge from the Immortal Man of Light to help continue the master plan.

I also found other ideas that were strikingly similar to those within the *Genesis* creation story. For instance, the Gnostic story explained that Adam and Eve were also warned not to eat from the Tree of Knowledge, and that they were similarly 'tricked' into eating its fruit by the serpent-beast.

However, what really captured my imagination was that the Gnostic story explained just who the serpent-beast was; the brother of Eve (the son of Eve of Life), the one who was left to roam in Paradise to continue the master plan. The author of the story even provided a telling description of a meeting between the siblings:

The wisest of all creatures came, the one they called Beast. When he saw how much Eve looked like their mother, Eve of Life, he said to her, "What lies did the Authorities tell you? Did they say do not eat from the Tree of Knowledge?"[3]

The Beast even explained to Eve why the Authorities did not want her to eat from the Tree of Knowledge; so they could hold on to the secret knowledge, maintain power and ultimately rule over the inhabitants of Paradise:

It was pure jealousy why the Authorities told you this, they did not want you to eat from the Tree of Knowledge.[4]

When Adam and Eve eventually ate from the Tree of Knowledge, the Authorities came rushing to see the effect, and when questioned Eve replied:

The Instructor, my brother, urged me on to eat from the tree...[5]

On seeing the strange effect of the tree on Adam, the Authorities reacted in fear, and in a collective voice exclaimed:

> Look at Adam! He is now like one of Us, he knows the difference between the light and the darkness, the good and the evil.[6]

Realising that this event was also critical to the *Genesis* story, I turned to my Bible, to see if there was any mention of the Authorities (*Genesis* 3:22):

> And the Lord God said, "Behold, the man has become as one of Us to know good and evil."

The Fall, the Griffin and the Tree of Life

Out of all the comparative ideas that I discovered, I believe the one concerning the Tree of Life was the most significant. For instance, just like God, the Authorities realised that with their new-found knowledge, from the Tree of Knowledge, and immortality from the Tree of Life, Adam and Eve would have the ability to challenge their rule in Paradise:

> ...just like with the Tree of Knowledge, they will go to the Tree of Life and eat the fruit and become immortal. With the true knowledge of the gods and immortality they will certainly hate us, seeing just what we are! They will attempt to overthrow Us and our Kingdom[7].

Inevitably, for their own self-preservation, the Authorities had to stop Adam and Eve from accessing Paradise. So, just like God in the *Genesis* story, they cast Adam and Eve to earth, taking steps to, not only guard the gateway to Paradise, but also the way to the Tree of Life. Here the Authorities, just like God:

> ...surrounded the Tree of Life with monstrous, fearful things, creatures called Cherubin, and they put a flaming sword with them, turning all the time, so that no being from the earth might ever be able to access Paradise.[8]

I could not quite work out why Yaltabaoth/God and the Authorities wanted to guard the gateway to Paradise and the Tree of Life. If Adam and Eve had been cast to earth, how could they have possibly found their way back to Paradise as mortals? It then suddenly came to me that there could only be one answer to all this: Yaltabaoth/God and the Authorities must have known that it was somehow possible for the mortals to find their way back to Paradise.

When I turned back to the Gnostic story, I was immediately faced with a physical description of the celestial entities that were used to guard the gateway to Paradise and the Tree of Life. These Cherubin, or "Cherubim" in *Genesis*, were described as strange hybrid creatures, made-up of eight shapes, as follows:

> The Cherubin has eight different shapes for each of the four corners, a mix of lion, calf, human and eagle forms.[9]

Fascinated by what the eight shapes of the Cherubin might look like, I started trawling the internet, looking for more detailed descriptions. I soon found that they could be half-

Figure 7

human and half-bull, or half-lion and half-human etc.[10] But of all the Cherubin combinations on offer, the one that interested me the most was the one containing the body of a lion and the head of an eagle. This particular form was the same as the mythical griffins, alongside the rabbits, which were *guarding the tree* on the misericord at St. Mary's in Beverley (fig. 7).

Intrigued by this connection, I took the time to look into the nature of the griffin, and quickly found a definition that confirmed my suspicions:

> Due to its association with immortality, the treasures guarded by griffins are the Tree of Life and the road to salvation. [11]

Satisfied that the misericord was representing the religious or possibly Gnostic idea of Cherubins guarding the Tree of Life, my attention switched to the rabbits. I suppose I was drawn to the rabbits for obvious reasons, but mostly because of George's strange comment about their esoteric nature; in that they were a metaphor for the human race, which held within its very essence the keyword for unlocking God's secret knowledge.

Realising that I was now working in uncharted territory, I picked up the phone again and gave the Oracle a ring.

I explained my latest findings to George, but at first he was non-comitial.

"Have you got a picture of the Ripon White Rabbit to hand?" George eventually asked.

Luckily I had my computer switched on and double-clicked the folder containing the image. As the familiar composition appeared on screen a sudden chill passed over me.

Figure 6

"So, Richard, why do you think the guardian-griffin is attacking the White Rabbit?" he asked.

"I suppose he must be protecting the way to the Tree of Life?"

"So if we were the White Rabbit and we had somehow found the keyword to unlock God's secret knowledge, then what's left to do?"

Working through the conundrum, I slowly replied, "Take from the Tree of Life... become immortal... challenge the Authorities and regain our Paradise."

"Bravo. That's right. This is why the White Rabbit, as the universal icon for the quest to regain Paradise, was not only used by early cultures, but also by the medieval artisans, the Rosicrucians and ultimately by Lewis Carroll in his story."

The Beast – We've Got Your Number

It was around a month after I had finished reading the Gnostic creation story that I received some junk email, which was sent by a company that operates several high-profile gambling websites, including 888.com. As was the norm with such emails I deleted it, but at the same time I was aware that I had seen '888' somewhere before, in a different setting.

Late that evening I set-about trawling through my files until I found what I was looking for, an old folder entitled *Numerology*. Clicking on the sub-folder entitled *888*, I began to remember that the number had been used by the Greeks to represent, not only the 'higher mind', but also the name of the Christian messiah, Jesus.[12] Even though I found all this fascinating, it was only when I had knocked back my last mouthful of wine that it suddenly came to me; there was another number, a number for another important biblical character, 666, the number of the Beast.

Well aware of the significance of the Beast to the Gnostic master plan, I turned to the final, sixty-sixth book of the Bible, the *Book of Revelation*, which talks about his number:

Here is wisdom. Let him who has understanding calculate the number of the beast, for it is the number of a man, his number is 666.

Considering that this number might also relate to a name, as with the Jesus example, I started a search. But after twenty minutes or so trawling the internet, it became apparent that it did not have a basis in Greek, Hebrew or even Arabic numerology. In fact, I found little evidence to suggest that the number had been based on any numerological system at all.

I decided to take another approach, focussing on the idea that it was only those with "understanding" who could "calculate" the Number of the Beast. In an attempt to solve this seemingly ancient mathematical puzzle, I promptly multiplied the numbers together (6X6X6) and then typed the result (216) into a search engine. I then clicked on a link to a Wikipedia site that was dedicated to the number 216, which also talked about its relationship to the Beast.[13] Even though it seemed like a long shot, I turned again to the Bible, to see if 216 corresponded to any sort of numerical reference. Hoping that it would provide some information about the nature of the Instructor-Beast or events surrounding the master plan and the Tree of Knowledge, I flipped over the pages until I came to the only feasible reference, *Genesis* 2:16:

And the Lord God [Authorities] Commanded the man, saying, "Of every tree in the garden you may freely eat; but of the Tree of the Knowledge of good and evil you shall not eat, for in the day that you eat of it you shall surely die."

4th Degree

Past Masters

In an attempt to uncover the origins of the Gnostic quest to regain Paradise, I turned to other more ancient cultures, reading through some of the earliest stories known to human kind; stories that were written around BC 3500 in Mesopotamia, the so-called cradle of civilisation. However, it was only when I discovered that some of these stories were strikingly similar to the *Genesis* account of creation that I knew I was onto something.[1]

The Annuna and the Tree of Life

After several weeks of searching, I found a story called *Adapa and the Food of Life*,[2] which not only holds a description of the Mesopotamian version of creation, but also a detailed account of the celestial entities that make-up the so-called Mesopotamian *Annuna* or 'god system'. Here the supreme god, Anu, just like the Immortal Man of Light, was in charge of the entire show. While the so-called gods of heaven and earth, just like Yaltabaoth and his Authorities, were in charge of creating the first man, in this case Adapa.

According to the story, Adapa, the original mortal hero, initially took-up residence in southeast Mesopotamia, on the Persian Gulf, and was left there to make bread, fish and tend the first earthly temple. Unfortunately, one day while out fishing the strength of the wind forced Adapa's boat to capsize, and in an extraordinary act he decided to break one of the 'wings' of the wind. The great god Anu took note of the drying-effect this had on the land and in turn summoned Adapa to Paradise, to the House of Anu. Interestingly, before Adapa set-off for the House of Anu, his God father, Ea, gave him some very familiar deceitful advice, in hope that he would not take the 'food of life' and become immortal:

Food of death they will set before thee, Eat not.[3]

As part of his talk to Adapa, Ea also explained:

When to heaven thou has ascended, and has approached the gate of Anu, the bearers of life at the gate of Anu will be standing.[4]

I knew that the idea of two entities 'bearing the food of life' at the gateway to a celestial realm featured in both the *Genesis* and Gnostic creation stories. So I began looking for information about the Mesopotamian 'bearers of life', to see if they were in any way comparable to the griffins or Cherubins that guarded the way to the Tree of Life. To my delight, I found that these Mesopotamian entities, Tammuz and Gishzida, were guardians of the Mesopotamian Tree of Life.[5] Further still, while attempting to find a depiction of entities, I discovered an image of them guarding the way to the Tree of Life,[6] which I immediately compared to the misericord carving from St. Mary's (fig. 11).

Figure 11

The Caduceus and the Tree of Life

Not having seen George for a couple of months, I took what I had found to his shop. As soon as I mentioned Mesopotamia and Tammuz and Gishzida his eyes lit up, and he made his way over to one of the sagging bookshelves in the corner of the room. As he was thumbing his way along the titles he began shouting out.

"You've unearthed a good example of the quest to regain Paradise in Mesopotamia. You will now have to shed your skin and look for the serpent."

Having no idea what he was talking about, I just waited for a more detailed explanation, which eventually came in the form of an open book that he pushed into my chest. When I looked down, I saw a large picture of an ambulance.

Not knowing what to make of the modern image I simply asked, "What?"

George tapped the page with the tip of his gnarled fingernail.

"Look for the snake."

Doing as he asked, I saw the snake on the side of the ambulance, which was wrapped around a central pole.

He then placed another book over the first, which held what looked like an image of a carving from the front of an ancient temple, containing two snakes, again wrapped around a central wooden pole or trunk. After a few moments of silence George leaned in.

"This snake-inspired symbol is a depiction of the wand of Hermes or the caduceus, which in the past was used by many civilisations to signify immortality. It was eventually adopted by physicians as their symbol, due to its historical association with the power of healing. If you can find the origins of the caduceus all will be revealed."

When I got back home I set about looking into the origins of this unusual symbol. Almost straight away I found that the caduceus appeared in many diverse settings, such as Aztec paintings, modern medical jewellery and old works on Hermetic alchemy (fig. 12).[7]

Figure 12

I also discovered a very early example of the caduceus on a ritual-cup, which was given to a Mesopotamian king around BC 3000 (fig. 13).[8]

Figure 13

As you can see from the drawing of the detail that surrounds the cup (right), two griffin-type creatures are guarding the caduceus. The Mesopotamian cup also holds an inscription, which reads:

> To the god Ningizzida, his god Gudea... for the prolongation of his life, has dedicated this.

The god Ningizzida was one of the Mesopotamian gods of heaven and earth; but what I found most interesting, when looking-up the role of Ningizzida, was that he was also known as Lord of the Tree of Life,[9] and that the caduceus-griffin seal on the cup was a depiction of the Tree of Life being protected.

I also discovered that Ningizzida was adopted by the Egyptians and renamed Thoth,[10] so I decided to get hold of a picture of Thoth to see how the Egyptians depicted him. As

Figure 14

you can see in the drawing by the eminent Egyptologist, Wallis Budge (fig. 14), Thoth is holding a strange yet familiar looking object in his hand.

After researching the nature of this object, I found that, just like the Mesopotamian caduceus, it was symbolic of immortality, which in this case was reserved for the Egyptian gods.

I then contacted the British Museum with my research and a unique proposition. I received this tantalising reply around a week later from the Department of the Middle East:

Thank you for your email. I must say that you have spotted something that is really very interesting. Even though I have much expertise in the field of comparative iconography, I had never noticed it before. I feel that I have to agree with you; the object in Thoth's hand is highly comparable to Ningizzida's

Figure 15

seal containing the caduceus. The symbol at the centre of Thoth's object, the *Ankh* or 'Anch' (the symbol for immortality) is indeed the Egyptian equivalent of the caduceus. And both do appear to be supported by griffin-like creatures. Of course, since Thoth was the equivalent of Ningizzida in ancient lore, it all makes perfect sense. In fact I have no trouble with the idea that Thoth's object is an interpretation of the earlier Ningizzida seal for the Tree of Life. I have attached an image of the Anch, which looks as if it were directly inspired by the caduceus [fig. 15]. The Anch is formed here using the snake, which is coiled around what is known as a tau cross. Hope this is of use to you.

(Reply: Department of the Middle East)

I also took the time to carefully follow the evolution of Ningizzida through the ages, and found that his Egyptian successor, Thoth, was eventually renamed Hermes Trismegistus by the Greeks.[11] Hermes Trismegistus was not only revered by many of the early Eastern mystery schools, but was, in the 17th century, revered by the Rosicrucian Order.[12] As you can see in the relatively well-known Rosicrucian-inspired etching of Hermes Trismegistus (fig. 16),[13] he is depicted alongside the original Mesopotamian symbol for the Tree of Life, the caduceus.

Figure 16

Figure 17

While trying to get to the bottom of the origins of the 'immortal symbolism' attached to the coiled-snakes, I found that the Rosicrucians had been well aware of its ancient status. In fact, I rediscovered an interesting example of it on the title page of a work that I already knew, *New Atlantis* (fig. 17), which was written by the Rosicrucian Grand Master, Francis Bacon. That is, the work which talks about the college intent on unlocking God's secret knowledge for the benefit of humankind.[14] As you can see, the snake here is not actually coiled around a tau cross, but a tau-like anchor.

Now, I am sure that most people will be unaware that the early Egyptian Christians did not use the cross as their prime religious symbol. What they actually used was the Anch.[15] In fact, the Anch was the symbol of the early Egyptian Christians until the rise of the Coptic Church in the latter half of the 1st century AD.

When I eventually got round to debating this issue with George, he came up with a very interesting proposition.

"In the early years of Egyptian Christianity, the idea of discarding the sacred symbol of the Anch did not go down well with the Gnostic-Christians. Instead of giving it up, they did the next best thing; they transformed the Anch into a Christian symbol. To this end, they created what is now the second most important symbol in Christendom, the symbol of Hope. Today we know it as the 'Anch-or' or anchor." (fig. 18).

Figure 18

George continued to build on his idea.

"The early Gnostic-Christians were aware of the true significance of the anchor, in that it was inspired by the more ancient caduceus, which symbolised the power of immortality that was contained within the Tree of Life." (fig. 19).

Figure 19

"So this all relates to the symbol that appears on the front of *New Atlantis* George?"

"Of course it does. This is why Francis Bacon used the Gnostic anchor of Hope with the snake. He used it to not only portray our deep seated urge to gain salvation through the immortal powers of the Tree of Life, but also to highlight the timing of an archaic prophesy associated with the quest to regain Paradise."

"An archaic prophesy?"

"Yes. A prophesy concerning the unknown adepts that will one day begin the process of regaining Paradise."

"So where can I find a copy of this prophesy then George?"

He stood up and made his way over to the glass-fronted unit at the back of the shop, which I knew held a selection of rare and expensive books. Before he reached it he stopped.

"No, it is not the right time, you're not ready."

On seeing the sincerity in his eyes, I decided not to challenge him.

"Well, if you say so George."

"Now I know this might sound a little stupid, no, ridiculous, but I once thought that I was one of the prophesised adepts. It cost me dearly. In fact, I am now starting to think that I have made a mistake with you. I should not have invited you to play this dangerous game. Life is too precious to waste."

"Dangerous game?"

"Yes, dangerous. It might all seem very provocative now, but like the search for Pandora's Box, the Arc of the Covenant or even the Fountain of Youth, the quest to regain Paradise has consumed the life of many seemingly discerning individuals."

"So you're saying that a quest to regain Paradise really exists; people have actually attempted to regain it?"

George moved towards the window and wiped away the condensation.

"Why do you think people like us crave to find a truth that is not in the day-to-day beauty of life, but in the intangible, in the deepest recesses of the esoteric mysteries?"

"I'm not sure George. I suppose many people get their

kicks from pursuing the darker side of mystery. For me, it is the unknown, the chance to unearth something that will thrill me to the core."

"No. It's because we are lonely. We chase mystery in an attempt to give our lives meaning and significance, because we crave to be part of something that is beyond life itself."

"But what of the world without a sense of mystery George?"

"I'll tell you what, have a think about what I've said, and if you do truly want to follow the White Rabbit to the source, I will not stand in your way. You may also want to consider that there are others out there that will do anything to get their hands on information pertaining to the quest, using both fair and foul means."

"Give over George, don't be so melodramatic."

"As you wish. But remember, I have warned you."

"Indeed you have."

5th Degree

The Druid Secret

After a couple of weeks thinking about George's 'warning', I began to realise that something was missing. The wheels of mystery were still working hard in my mind, but I was travelling down the metaphorical road to nowhere. So putting his words to the back of my mind, I got in the car and headed out for the Old Vicarage. On my arrival at the bookshop, I saw that George was busy talking to a colourfully dressed woman, so I decided not to interrupt and began browsing through his recent book acquisitions, which were piled on his desk.

"So do you regret ruffling the feathers of the Supreme Council of Antiquities?" I heard George ask.

"What's important is that I found the prize, undoubtedly Nefertiti. She was absolutely beautiful, very well preserved. I couldn't really ask for more."

George looked at me and winked.

"Now then Ricardo, we are in the presence of giants. We have our very own Egyptologist here with us today."

She smiled.

"So, it's been entertaining as usual George, but I have to go up to the museum now to sort out a collection. Go easy on him, he looks a little green."

As the woman left the shop I frowned. Laughing, George casually opened his desk drawer, took out a folded piece of paper and passed it to me.

"So you want to see just how far the rabbit hole goes then?"

Dismissing the comment, I unfolded the grubby specimen and saw that he had written down two references, the first being to a 16th century book called *Camdeni Britannia*.

"This book holds an important description of the ancient realm of Brigantia." George slid his finger down to the second reference. "And this is for a book called *Uriel's Machine*, which will be a little easier to source. These references will put you on the trail of the Druid's pyramid-temple secret."

"So what about the quest to regain Paradise?"

"Well, the Druids of Ancient Albion were the ones who instigated the quest. They were the first to discover and use the keyword to unlock God's secret knowledge; knowledge containing the divine blueprint for building the temple-gateway to access the celestial realm."

"A temple-gateway to Paradise? That's a beauty George."

"Yes, and all you have to do now is find it."

The Pyramid-Henge Orion Mystery

Having waited for the relevant librarian to return from lunch, I eventually settled down to a copy of *Camdeni Britannia*, which had been locked away in the Strong Room at York Library.[1] I turned to the section on the ancient realm of Brigantia, as suggested by George, and soon discovered that it was the old name for the realm

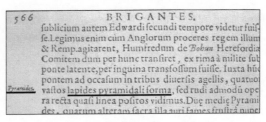

Figure 20

that once covered much of the now County of Yorkshire. What jumped out at me, as I worked through the familiar place-names in Brigantia, was the strange reference to "Pyramides" and the objects described as 'stone Pyramid forms'. I have underlined the Latin words in question (fig. 20).

On the following Sunday morning, late on in May, 2003, I invited my dad, a veteran of many a mystery quest, to join me in a search for "Pyramides". Based on clues from *Camdeni Britannia*, which hinted at the location of the pyramid forms, we first visited Devil's Arrows in Knaresborough. After a conversation with a doctor walking his dog, we were then directed to the nearby triple henge-system at Thornborough, North Yorkshire.

"Yes, pyramids," the doctor said, scratching his head. "I don't know where I heard it, but I am sure I was once told a tale about the henges at Thornborough being linked to the pyramids. I may be wrong, but it's the best I can do for you chaps."

All that is left of the Thornborough henge-system now is three massive, circular mounds, which are broken at the top and bottom by equal gaps (fig. 21). As you can see with help from the artistic bird's eye view of the system (left), my dad, Raymond (right), is standing inside the central henge, pointing out.

On our walk across the mile-long complex, we soon came across a group of strange looking people that were sitting on the floor.

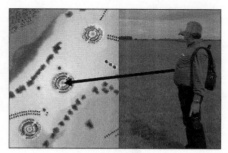

Figure 21

"Would you like to join in with our belated Beltane celebrations?" one of them asked. When I enquired as to what he was talking about, I had no idea that I had set myself up for a lecture on Druid rituals. So over the following hour or so, while my dad went off in search of rare fungi, I learnt all about the Druid seasons and even had a symbol painted on my forehead, in green. Towards the end of the lecture, one of the members of the group began questioning me.

"So what brought you here to Thornborough then?"

"We are in search of Pyramides."

One of the young women in the group looked at me.

"Are you aware of the connection between the three henges here at Thornborough and the three pyramids at Giza, in Egypt?"

"No, but it sounds fascinating."

She stood up, took my arm and led me away from the group, gesturing for me to join her on a broken mound that formed one of the henges.

"Just like the Pyramids at Giza, the henges at Thornborough were set-out to track the gradual shift in position of the sun over the solar year."

"So why would the ancient Druids and Egyptians want to do this?"

"Well, both cultures used the sun's subtle change in movement over the solar year to predict the change in seasons. In the case of the Thornborough henges, wooden stakes would have been driven into the curved mounds to track the sun's movement, whereas the change in the shadows cast by the pyramids would have provided the same information."

"So you're saying that both were acting as astronomical calendars?"

"Yes, exactly, but there is a more profound connection between the two calendar systems. The pyramids at Giza and the henges at Thornborough were both laid-out in the same celestial format to mimic the three main stars in Orion's belt."

"Do you have any proof of all this?"

"Actually, it was something that my grandfather told me just before he passed away."

Unfortunately this brought an uneasy end to our conversation, so I sheepishly thanked her for her time, waved to the group, and headed off to find my dad.

Inspired by the young woman's theory, and its possible connection to George's idea of a 'druidical temple-pyramid secret', I set-about looking for an astronomical connection between the pyramids and the Thornborough henges. Almost straight away, I found that the theory regarding the pyramids and the three stars in Orion's belt was put forward by a Belgium engineer called Robert Bauval, in the guise of a bestselling book called *The Orion Mystery*. When I acquired a copy of the book, the first thing I did was look for any mention of the Thornborough henges, but there wasn't one, so I decided to carry out a comparative study of my own. Basically, I examined three distinct yet similar images (fig. 22).

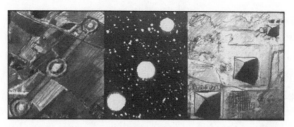

Figure 22

The central image in Figure 22 depicts the three main stars in Orion's belt, which Bauval suggested inspired the Egyptians to lay out their three pyramids (right). Similarly, the photograph of the Thornborough henge-system (left), shows that its layout mirrors the stars in Orion's belt; one being above (in the heavens), and the other below (on the earth). Convinced that I was onto something, I contacted Mr. Bauval through his website, to ask his opinion. Even though I did eventually receive a reply, I'm not sure it came directly from him, but it did serve to open up a new line of enquiry:

> Thanks for your email. Yes, it does seem like you are onto something here. Did you know that the Thornborough henge-system is seen by many as the most important prehistoric site between Stonehenge and the Orkneys? What I would focus on is the fact that the Thornborough system has been dated to around BC 3500. Good luck.

Well aware that the Egyptian pyramid system was constructed around BC 2500, this meant that the Thornborough system predated the pyramids by a thousand years. In other words, if there was anything to the idea that the ancients laid-out their 'astro-temples' to mirror Orion's belt, then it would have been the henge-builders of prehistoric Britain who first came up with the idea.[2] But what really got me thinking about all this was one of my dad's off-the-cuff remarks. He suggested that the Egyptians might have been taught this astronomical concept by the Druids from northern Britain. I must admit, I thought this idea was a little far-fetched, but then I looked into George's second reference, *Uriel's Machine*.

Enoch and Uriel's Machine

Uriel's Machine[3] is a controversial work by the academic, Yorkshire-based 'mystery' writers, Christopher Knight and Robert Lomas, which deals with a strange connection between the prehistoric henge-builders of Ancient Britain and an ancient book called the *Book of Enoch*.[4]

The character Enoch, from the *Book of Enoch*, lived in Ancient Mesopotamia around BC 3500, and the book describes his miraculous journey with an archangel to acquire God's secret knowledge; knowledge that would be of great relevance to a future generation:

I saw the vision of the Holy One in the heavens, which the angels showed me, and from them I heard everything, and from them I understood as I saw, but not for this generation, but for a remote one which is for to come.[5]

As part of his journey, Enoch was also taken to a place in the "North", where he was shown a special astronomical device consisting of what he described as three portals of heaven:

And from thence I went towards the North to the ends of the earth, and there I saw a great and glorious device... And here I saw three portals of heaven open in the heavens [where] there is cold, hail, frost, snow, dew, and rain.[6]

Immediately I thought of the three henges at Thornborough. But could Enoch have visited Thornborough in BC 3500 to see the three mysterious portals of heaven? Enter the academics, Knight and Lomas.

The authors named their work *Uriel's Machine* after Archangel Uriel, who in the *Book of Enoch* guided Enoch on his journey to the North to acquire God's secret knowledge. Their book focuses on the idea that the device or machine that Uriel showed to Enoch was a massive, wooden solar-henge for calculating the change in seasons over the solar year. From information contained within the *Book of Enoch*, the academics were able to reproduce the machine, so I decided to see if it was in any way comparable to the henges at Thornborough.

To my astonishment, when I eventually drew out the machine, using the *Book of Enoch* and Knight and Lomas' findings (fig. 23, left), and placed it alongside one of the Thornborough henges (right), I saw that they were both broken circles with equal gaps. And that Uriel's Machine

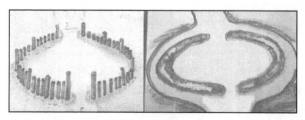

Figure 23

held the all-important wooden stakes needed to form the solar henges.

Knight and Lomas also analysed the 'effect of the sun' on Uriel's Machine (from the *Book of Enoch*), to determine just where the machine had been built. They concluded that it was situated between latitudes 51 and 59 degrees north. Again, to my astonishment, when I looked on a map, I realised that the Thornborough henge-system sat at the centre of these two points, around 54 degrees north (fig. 24).

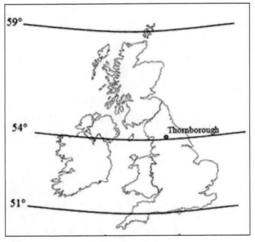

Figure 24

Enoch's Passage of Knowledge

Having read *Uriel's Machine* thoroughly, I again found no reference to the Thornborough henge-system. So I began searching for other stories that might reveal a little more about Enoch's journey to the North. Here I discovered an interesting legend that appears within various secret society teachings, which is generally referred to as the *Legend of Enoch's Temple*.

According to the Speculative Freemasonic (Freemasonry) version of this legend,[7] when Enoch eventually took possession of God's secret knowledge, he soon-after built a subterranean temple to keep it safe. But what really excited me about this legend was the description of the location of Enoch's Temple, since it stated that the temple was constructed under the sacred mount that later housed King Solomon's Temple.

In an attempt to get to the bottom of this interesting 'coincidence', I called in a favour from an old friend who was a member of a Masonic lodge in York. He was keen to chat and invited me to a doubles match at the Stonebow Snooker Club with a couple of his brethren. Here we discussed the issue of the *Legend of Enoch's Temple* between frames, and by the end of the evening I had been kindly offered access to their Masonic library.

As I recall it was a Wednesday evening when I met with the lodge archivist. I must admit I was a little nervous when I knocked on the lodge door, but after a warm welcome I soon settled down. We then made our way down towards the library.

"John, your friend, explained that you are not a Mason, so what's your interest with the legend of Enoch, if you don't mind me asking?"

I quickly explained about my dealings with George and the mystery surrounding the quest to regain Paradise. I could see the archivist was amused by what I had to say, but also intrigued, because he kept stopping along the way to clarify his thoughts. Just before we entered the library he paused for a final time.

"Did you know that in the *Book of Enoch*, Enoch is taken to see the Tree of Life?"

Not being aware of this, I promised that I would look into the issue when I got back home.

Once inside the library he pointed me in the direction of a manuscript and a couple of old looking books that he must have laid out earlier.

"I think it is also worth mentioning that Enoch, the Keeper of Knowledge, has been identified with the Egyptian Thoth."

"What Hermes Tismigistus?"

"Yes, just type Thoth Enoch Hermes into the net and you will find detailed files. In fact, some scholars suggest that the Egyptians used Enoch's knowledge to build the pyramids in Egypt. Masonic Scholars from the last century even suggest that the pyramids were built by Enoch himself, before the reign of Pharaoh Kufu. One of the books I have laid out for you explains all this. But this old copy of Mr. Wood's manuscript from 1610 holds one of the earliest surviving versions of the Ancient Charges of Freemasonry. I believe the original manuscript is held at the Provincial Grand Lodge Library in Worcestershire. It also states that Enoch's secret knowledge was eventually passed on to the Egyptians."

As he left the room and closed the door I felt like a child in a candy shop. I turned to the copy of the Wood manuscript[8] and read about the passage of Enoch's knowledge to the Egyptians. I then read through the section in the old book which explained that Enoch was responsible for constructing the Great Pyramid at Giza.[9] While considering the implications of this apparent 'passage of knowledge', I found myself thinking about the young woman's idea, in that the pyramids were constructed to act as a solar calendar, just like the henges at Thornborough and Uriel's Machine. It then started to dawn on me that if the Egyptians had used Enoch's secret knowledge, which he had gathered from the North, then it would explain why the pyramids were designed to perform the same solar-function as the henges. Moreover, it would also explain why the Thornborough henge-system and the Giza pyramid-system were both laid out to mimic the stars in Orion's belt; because they were both based on God's 'secret astronomical knowledge'.

When the archivist returned, I explained my ideas about Enoch's passage of knowledge. I could tell that he was intrigued because he pushed out his lower lip, frowned and then settled into a chair.

"You may be right. I suppose there is always a little truth to every legend. The Enoch-character could have been a metaphor for an early group of Mesopotamian explorers, who at some point in the distant past travelled to the North, possibly Thornborough. I suppose these explorers would have almost certainly found Druid-type communities, which not only held strange religious beliefs, but also detailed knowledge about henge-construction techniques."

"So do you think that these Mesopotamian explorers might have taken the Druids' knowledge back home and used it to develop their own ideas, ideas that were later adopted by other cultures in the area such as the Egyptians?"

"Well I believe that you now have much evidence to support the idea that the underlying blueprint for building astro-religious temples arcs back to the Druids of Albion. But what you have to remember is that allegory plays an important role, in fact an intrinsic role in the search for enlightenment. Anyway, if you need any more help just let me know. I have really enjoyed revisiting this fascinating subject. In a way you remind me of myself when I first set out to unravel the mysteries of the ancients."

Yggdrasil and the Tree of Life

Later that week I left work early and headed back to the bookshop. When I arrived George was in the middle of an argument with a young man. At first I could not quite work out what it was all about, but as I listened in it seemed to be based around the comics that were strewn across his desk. Not wanting to get involved, I began looking across the titles on the bookshelves, until I arrived at the window with a view of the entrance to the indoor market.

As I gazed down to see if there was anything going on in the car park, I noticed a piece of paper on the windowsill with a strange word scrawled across it. Unaware that the argument had ended and the man had left the shop, I proceeded to pick up the piece of paper and began trying to pronounce the word, rolling my lips round and sticking my tongue out like a deranged baboon. As I had just about got my lips around the word, I heard it dance through the air in a melodious tone, as if it had somehow come to life.

"Yggdrasil."

George quickly apologised for the earlier commotion and took the piece of paper from my hand.

"I assume you have made some progress?"

I gave him a detailed account of my findings and told him about the discussion I had with the Masonic archivist.

"You are sort of on the right track," George proposed. "But you should have picked-up on the clue that the archivist gave to you."

I was aware that he was unlikely to explain straight away what it was.

"So what's this Yggdrasil thing then George?"

"That's it, the Tree of Life, the Yggdrasil, that's what the archivist was hinting at."

"Yggdrasil means Tree of Life?"

"To truly understand the origins of the forever-green, yew tree Yggdrasil will take you one step closer to the treasure."

"But what about the temple, the portal, the gateway and stuff?"

"Be patient, follow the mystery as it unfolds. You have the gateway in your sights, don't you?"

"I suppose so."

"Then don't fret, seek the Yggdrasil."

When I got back home, I typed Yggdrasil into a search engine, but it took several weeks of research to work out just what George was talking about, as I will explain.

Imagine a country churchyard, on a winter's day. Here the snow is falling, and the first thing you notice is the naked, lifeless branches of an old oak tree. You then turn and see a dark-green mass that is quickly turning to white. What you are most probably looking at is the evergreen yew tree. I say this because there is much archaeological evidence to suggest that many of the Christian-Saxon and later medieval churches were built on Pagan or Druid sites.[10] To this end, it is postulated that the Druids initially chose these sites because of the presence of sacred, evergreen yew trees, which still remain there today.[11]

Why the yew tree was so special to the early British-Druid cultures is not so straight forward, but many suggest that it had something to do with the tree's immortal-like qualities.[12] For instance, one of the most interesting facts about the yew tree is that, as it dies, a new tree emerges from its rotten core or root-bole, making it a seemingly immortal tree. I also found that the yew was seen as a sacred tree by many other Pagan cultures from the Northern Hemisphere, including the Greeks and North American Indians.[13] Here the beautiful fragrant vapour from its heated resin was inhaled, since it held what they believed were mystical healing properties. But probably the best example of the evergreen yew tree, as a mystical tree, appears in Norse mythology, where it features as the *Yggdrasil* or 'Yew tree-column'. To this end, the Yggdrasil gained a generic name that has been used throughout the ages, the Tree of Life.[14] Moreover, people have suggested that the Yggdrasil is synonymous with the Tree of Life that appears in the Near East creation stories;[15] the tree that would give us immortality and the means by which to challenge the Authorities in Paradise.

To further explore this intriguing connection, I kept my promise to the archivist and turned to the *Book of Enoch*, to see if I could find the episode where he was taken to see the Tree of Life. Again, I read through all the astronomical secrets that had been given to Enoch, until I reached the episode in question. Here I found that Enoch had been taken to see the Tree of Life by an Archangel, who explained all about its immortalising properties. But what really caught my imagination was Enoch's own description of the Tree of Life:

> ...it had a fragrance beyond all fragrance, and its leaves and blooms and wood wither not forever.[16]

I do agree that it is a matter of interpretation, but for me, Enoch's description of the Tree of Life seemed very similar to the folklore-properties attributed to the yew tree. That is, a tree which lived forever, emitted fragrant healing vapours, and was indeed referred to as the Tree of Life. All this seemed to make sense at the time, since I was caught-up with the idea that the ancient Druids of Britain had influenced other ancient cultures across the globe. However, what I didn't realise was that I had inadvertently discovered a connection that would lead me to the druidical capital of Ancient Britain, Eborakon; the place that holds the temple-gateway that was built to give the prophesised adepts access to Paradise.

6th Degree

The Key Word of God

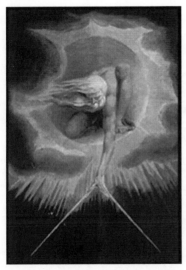

Figure 25

In an attempt to corroborate the radical idea that the Albion Druids' knowledge about temple architecture had influenced the early Mesopotamians and later Egyptians, I eventually turned to stories describing the most ancient of all architects, God himself. Here I found that secret societies, both past and present, had described God as the Great Architect or Geometrician of the Universe.[1] As you can see with the enigmatic painting by William Blake (fig. 25), the Great Architect is hard at work with his divider, checking the 'squareness' of his creation.

Probably the best example of this Great Architect concept can be found in a set of questions from the biblical Old Testament, posed by God himself to a man called Job:

Where was thou when I laid the foundations of the earth?

Declare if though have understanding.

Who hath laid the measures of it, if though knowest?

Or who hath stretched the line upon it?[2]

This idea of laying the foundations of the earth, whilst "measuring" and "stretching the line upon it" inspired me to dig deeper, and I soon discovered that several Mesopotamian creation gods, such as Marduk and Nannar (fig. 26), were depicted with a measuring stick and a ring of chord for setting out the extent of their divine creations.

Figure 26

I even began to consider that the idea that gods 'ruled' had originated from this ancient measuring concept.

Laying the Foundations

To my delight, I discovered an example of this ancient cord-measuring concept in an episode from the *Book of*

Enoch, which appears to link to the construction of the northern solar henges:

> And I saw in those days how long cords were given to those angels and they took to themselves wings and flew, and they went towards the North. And I asked the angel, saying unto him: Why have those angels taken these cords and gone off? And he said unto me: They have gone to measure.[3]

Figure 27

I even found a Mesopotamian carving of this scene, within the Iraq Museum (fig. 27), depicting an angel with the rings of chord.

As part of my enquiry, I decided to see if the Egyptians had used this cord-measuring concept to help build their pyramids. The idea being that, if I could find evidence of it in Egypt, it would help to substantiate the idea from the Enoch legend. That is, the idea that Enoch's secret construction-knowledge from the North had been found and used by the Egyptians.

After some detailed research, I discovered that when the Ancient Egyptians built their temples and pyramids, they used a ritual called the "stretching of the chord ceremony";[4] a good example of which I found on the walls of the Temple of Amun-Re at Karnak. In this monumental ceremony, the goddess Sechat was responsible for helping the pharaoh align the new temple or pyramid by stretching-out the cord to the *east*, towards the so-called seventh star. As you can see in the Egyptian carving from Luxor (fig. 28), the goddess Sechat is taking measure, and her headdress holds the ancient hieroglyph for

Figure 28

the seventh star, which is made-up of seven rays.

Interestingly, the seventh star, Alcyone, is situated in a mystical cluster of seven stars called the Pleiades. In the time of the Egyptian Old Kingdom, the Pleiades consistently rose in the sky due-east, and Alcyone acted as the cord-stretching, celestial marker to align the new temple or pyramid to the east. While exploring this issue, I eventually telephoned a professor from the Department of Anthropology at Harvard University, who had a detailed understanding of this ancient concept.

"Yes, the Pleiades temple-alignment technique was also used by the Aztec pyramid builders," he explained. "Their Great Pyramid of the Sun at Teotihuacán, just outside Mexico City, was also aligned to the east to meet with the Pleiades. The Aztec king, just like the Egyptian pharaoh, was buried at the heart of the pyramid temple, until a time when he would be transported to the realm of the gods."

"So you are saying that the pyramid-temple acted as portal or gateway to access the realm of Paradise."

"Yes, in effect, the spiritual temple has always been seen as the link between heaven and earth in most cultures."

"This might sound strange, but could a mortal use the temple to access Paradise?"

"I'm not sure about that, but in Egypt this sort of thing became somewhat of a theme in the later dynasties. Rich people would commission a copy of the *Book of Emerging Forth into the Light*, the *Book of the Dead*, in hope that they would be able to follow various magic spells to help them navigate their way to the higher realm, just like the Pharaoh."

"You don't by any chance know about the three portals of heaven that Enoch saw? I believe this could tie in with the idea of the temple being a gateway."

"No, sorry, I can't help you with that one."

The Missing Druid Link

To bring some sort of resolution to my investigation, I began looking for descriptions of the use of the Pleiades alignment technique in the construction of the northern solar henges. I knew that if I could find direct evidence of this, it would give even more weight to the idea that the Druids' temple building techniques had been adopted by the Mesopotamians and later Egyptians.

It was in January, 2004, at a party on the Brodsworth Estate in South Yorkshire, when I made a significant breakthrough with this issue. To be honest I was not invited to the party, I sort of slipped in with my dad, who had been invited due to the research work he had carried out for the estate's chief trustee, Graciela Artola de Williams.

It was at the party that I got talking to a knowledgeable Mexican gentleman called Perez, about a recently discovered Aztec snake-temple that was aligned to the east, to the Pleiades star cluster. When I mentioned my theory about the alignment of the Druid's solar henges to the same star cluster, his eyes lit up.

"As it happens, I have something that might help to substantiate your theory."

He asked me to follow him into one of the large rooms across from the party, and offered me a slender chair that was situated next to an old walnut-veneered desk. After fumbling through a neat pile of magazines he found what he was looking for, the latest addition of the *National Geographic*. Flicking back and forth several times he suddenly stopped, folded back the pages and placed it on the desk.

"This article is based around the discovery of a Druid sky-disc, which was unearthed from a Bronze-Age site. As you can see, it holds a blueprint for building a solar henge."

As I observed the disc, I realised that it was a pocket-size model of Uriel's Machine, containing two curved bands to represent the movement of the sun throughout the solar year.

"The bands look just like the broken mounds at the Thornborough henge-system."

Perez ignored my comment.

"The internet site dedicated to the disc says that the seven stars in the blueprint represent the Pleiades star cluster."[5]

"So this would explain just how the Druids aligned their solar temples to the east. They used the Pleiades, just like the Egyptians."

He took out a piece of paper from the desk with two drawings on it; one of the sky disk and the other a drawing containing earthly and heavenly symbols[6] (fig. 29).

"What I find interesting, is that the Pleiades star cluster also appears prominently in Masonic art work. You see, just like in the sky-disc, the Pleiades star cluster always sits in-between the sun and moon." Perez slowly circled the comparable sun, moon and seven stars with his finger. "If you examine both images it is plain to see, they both hold the same ancient, astronomical arrangement."

Figure 29

He continued in a knowing tone. "It is not at first obvious, but the disc [left] and Masonic artwork [right] are telling the same story. The artwork symbolises events surrounding the rebuilding of King Solomon's Temple. While in the case of the blueprint, it is there to illustrate how to build a solar temple or henge."

"So Solomon's Temple was also aligned to the east? But do you think that the Masonic Order still understands the meaning of this artwork; in that it depicts how the temple should be aligned?"

"I was just about to ask you the same question."

We spent the next hour or so debating the issue.

When I got back home I set about looking into the nature of Masonic symbolism and ritual, beginning with the first Masonic degree of initiation, the First Degree. As part of the initiation ceremony a so-called tracing board is used, which not only represents the metaphorical rebuilding of Solomon's Temple, but also the building of a human temple by the Masonic candidate. I began to think about Solomon's Temple as a Gnostic metaphor for a living temple. As I continued to read through the discourse associated with the First Degree, I kept an eye out for any reference to the temple's orientation or alignment, just in case there was any mention of the cardinal point of east, and I was not disappointed:

> Sacred buildings from time immemorial, including the glorious temple of Solomon, have been oriented with the most scrupulous exactness.[7]

I turned to the picture of the tracing board associated with the degree and found several exciting clues (fig. 30).[8]

The first thing I noticed was the strange arrangement of the cardinal points around the edge of the tracing board, showing east in the usual position of north, which I assumed was there to indicate the orientation of the temple. I then noticed again the sun,

Figure 30

71

moon and cluster of seven stars. But what fascinated me the most was the ladder at the centre of the scene, which led to the star with seven rays, Alcyone, the seventh star.

Feeling that it was time to seek guidance, I took up the offer of the Masonic archivist and arranged to meet with him again after one of his lodge dinners at the Mucky Duck pub. I remember vividly that sitting in a pub with a man wearing a tuxedo was not what I had in mind, but my comment about the situation did help to break the ice before we got down to business.

After showing him all that I had discovered he sat back.

"The origins of Masonic symbolism are actually unknown to the Order, but what you have discovered most likely relates to the ancient art of temple building, both spiritual and perhaps physical. The ancestors of Freemasonry, the medieval-religious stonemasons, also aligned each of their spectacular Gothic Minsters and Cathedrals to the east, to mimic the holiest of all temples, Solomon's Temple."

Again, I told the archivist about the medieval artisans' apparent link to the quest to regain Paradise. He nodded.

"Yes, it could be argued that the essence of the Cathedral, the House of God, is linked to the Hermetic tradition of bringing heaven to earth, or as above, so below."

But what really struck a chord with me was his comment about the ladder in the tracing board, which led to the star with seven rays.

"It's representative of a ladder from the Bible, Jacob's Ladder, which provided a special link between heaven and earth. In the biblical story, Jacob had been guided by God to an ancient, derelict temple near to Jerusalem, possibly one of your henges, where he rested his head on one of its toppled stones, and in turn received his vision of the ladder. Jacob went on to rename the place of the temple, calling it Bethel, *Bethel* meaning 'the House of God'."

"So the ladder basically represents a stairway to heaven then?"

The archivist laughed.

"Ironically, Robert Plant said that his inspiration for the song *Stairway To Heaven* came from Lewis Spence's book on druidical magic in Ancient Britain."

"So do you think that the temple, whether physical, metaphorical or even spiritual could ever provide a link between heaven and earth?"

I could see that he was a little uncomfortable with the question because he was staring at me as if I had asked for his bank account details or some such like. He leaned in with his glass of whisky. "Only with Enoch's Stone can the candidate perfect the temple."

"Enoch's Stone?"

He immediately sat back and winced as the words passed over my lips. He then knocked back his whisky and stood up.

"I have to go now, but do let me know how you get on."

When I eventually took all this fascinating stuff to George, I think he must have turned into Archimedes or perhaps Brian Blessed. I say this because he began shouting out in a barbaric tone. "Eureka, eureka, you have found it. Only by unlocking God's secret knowledge using Enoch's Stone can the temple be built."

He then began to babble, as if he were arguing with an invisible third party. A little shocked by this strange display, I attempted to bring him back round.

"Enoch's Stone? God's secret knowledge? The temple?"

He reacted quite vigorously to my questions, and with what seemed like a bout of clarity put forward a strange question.

"How does a bird know how to build a nest?"

"Because it is written into its genes I suppose."

"That's right. But before we get into all this, you first have to seek-out Enoch's metaphorical Stone; it is where the keyword was first written down. Remember though, the stone is metaphorical because it is actually written into our own physical architecture, our genes if you like; our means by which to unlock God's secret knowledge."

Enoch's Stone and the Lost Word of God

It took most of the following week to uncover the mystery surrounding Enoch's Stone, which appears in numerous legends and stories that were written by Jewish and Arabic adepts.[9] Here the stone held upon its upper face the so-called Lost Word of God, in the form of a Tetragrammaton,[10] which could be decoded and used to perform miraculous deeds in God's name, just like Solomon's keyword.

I also stumbled onto another version of the legend in Albert Mackey's work of 1882, *The Symbolism of Freemasonry*. Here it stated that Enoch carved the Lost Word of God into a special stone and hid it within his subterranean temple, which was composed of nine descending arches. It also stated that, when King Solomon began building his temple (around BC 1000), he rediscovered the stone and became the guardian of the Lost Word, the keyword:

....the stone thus discovered by Solomon was the identical one that had been deposited in his secret vault by Enoch.[11]

When I read this, I felt like I was on the verge of piecing together a seemingly lost history, which had not only been encoded into metaphor and allegory, but also preserved and passed down throughout the ages. In this case a lost history surrounding the keyword for unlocking God's secret knowledge – knowledge that was somehow linked to the ancient art of temple building, and quite possibly to the quest to regain Paradise. I even began to imagine events surrounding this passage of knowledge across time and culture.

In the first instance I envisaged Enoch on his journey to the North, alongside angels holding measuring cords. I could see three wooden henges in the form of Orion's belt, aligned to the east, to a mystical cluster of seven lights in the night sky. My mind zipped forward to the Egyptian pyramid builders, who were stretching out their sacred cord towards the night sky, alongside Sechat and the seventh star. I then found myself looking over Temple Mount in Jerusalem, where King Solomon was pointing to the east, whilst directing the demonic-Genii to construct his miraculous temple. In the blink of an eye I was with the medieval artisans, admiring one of their marvellous east-facing edifices, which had been crafted out of stone, wood and metal. Finally, I was back in more familiar times, standing next to a Masonic candidate in a candle lit room, alongside astronomical images, temple geometry and architectural forms, receiving the wisdom of the ancients. I could even feel the candidate's confusion as the Master Mason paid homage to the strange entity called the Great Architect of the Universe.

Assuming that I had done enough with Enoch's Stone, I took all my findings to George.

"So do you now see how the Lost Word and Solomon's keyword are descriptions of the same thing? Both are metaphorical descriptions of the means by which to unlock God's secret knowledge, which was hidden and subsequently lost to us at the time of our celestial downfall, when we ate from the Tree of Knowledge."

"But have you any evidence of all this George?"

"Well, in a way, yes. But to understand this evidence, you will first have to rediscover just how the Lost Word, the keyword, is contained within us, within our genes. There is only one way to do this. You must succeed where almost everyone else has failed. You must unravel the mystery surrounding the Enoch's Stone's philosophical counterpart, the Philosophers' Stone."

The Lost Word of God in Us – The Philosophers Stone

I found the Philosophers' Stone a little tricky to deal with, to say the least. But I soon discovered that the 17th century philosophical alchemists had been attempting to complete what is called the Great Work.[12] To be honest, there are different theories regarding the nature of this alchemical work, but in short it was based around the quest to acquire and use the power of the Philosophers' Stone.[13] From what I could gather, the Philosophers' Stone was an alchemical version of the Enoch's Stone, since it contained within it the means by which to unlock God's secret knowledge.[14] I suppose it must be noted that in *Harry Potter and the Philosopher's Stone*, the stone is depicted as a lump of red crystal. However, as the name suggests, the stone was actually philosophical, as it could only be unlocked in the mind of the alchemist after going through a transmutation or spiritual change.[15]

Very few descriptions of the Philosophers' Stone have been put forward over the centuries. For me though, the most revealing description exists in an obscure Rosicrucian-alchemical work called *Atalanta Fugiens*,[16] which was produced in 1617 by Michael Mair, one of Francis Bacon's Rosicrucian adepts. It contains fifty emblems that basically describe philosophical alchemy; the twenty-first emblem depicting the Philosophers' Stone (fig. 31).

Figure 31

When I first saw the humans at the centre of the stone, I realised that, if the stone did contain God's secret knowledge, then it would have to be part of us, since we were depicted as part of the stone. I then turned to the divider, like the one held by William Blake's Great Architect, which he used to check the 'squareness' of his creation. I could see that the anonymous figure, like God, was checking the geometric proportions of the stone. I then turned to its accompanying geometric description:

Make of the man and woman a Circle, of that a Quadrangle, of this a Triangle, of the same a Circle and you will have the Stone of the Philosophers.[17]

My suspicions were confirmed; it clearly explained that the stone was composed of a fusion between the human form and geometry. In this case a circle, quadrangle (square) and triangle. It was at this juncture that a vague memory suddenly popped into my mind; a memory of a rainy Easter holiday in southern France, where I was watching a controversial documentary on German satellite television. The documentary was based around the political influence of the Seattle-based think tank called the Discovery Institute, which is known for its advocacy of 'intelligent design'.

If you are not aware of the intelligent design concept, it basically suggests that hidden within the mathematical construct of nature is evidence of a planned 'sacred geometry', which was apparently conceived by some sort of Great Architect. For me, intelligent design was a modern version of the Philosophers' Stone; a stone that represented the essence of God's secret geometric knowledge, which was hidden within nature, within us. I could now see that if someone could crack the geometric code of the Philosophers Stone, they would be able to gain access to God's secret knowledge.

Quite excited by my discovery, I phoned George to explain that I now understood just what the Philosophers' Stone was. But he seemed to ignore my words and began talking about something called the Temple of Heaven in Beijing.

"This temple was built around the all-important concept of bringing Heaven to Earth. If you take the time to study its architecture, you will find that it is composed of a square to represent Earth and a circle to represent Heaven."

He then began to babble again, and after a few moments came out with a strange but tantalising statement.

"The Lost Word has already been used to unlock God's secret knowledge, and the blueprint within it was used to build the prophesised temple. The temple now resides within the original and prophesised New Jerusalem."

"Do you mean Solomon's Temple George?"

"So you think that the original Jerusalem was built upon the so-called Holy Land?"

"Of course, that's what most people believe, isn't it?"

"Well, this maybe the case, but you will have to consult with William Blake about the issue. He wrote a strange poem about John Milton, the guy who gave us *Paradise Lost* and *Paradise Regained*. If you look to this poem, I am sure it will not only lead you to the original and prophesised New Jerusalem, but also to the temple itself."

The Temple and the Word

Caught-up in George's words, I soon after typed "Blake poem Milton" into a search engine, to see what would come up. Clicking on the first of many links, I discovered that Blake had written a poem about Milton, entitled, aptly, *Milton a Poem*. As part of the preface to this poem, he also produced a much shorter poem, entitled, *And did those feet in ancient time*.[1]

As I read on, I realised that Blake's words from this short poem had been used to form the hymn *Jerusalem*. So I took out my primary school hymn book, turned to *Jerusalem* and began looking on the internet for information about his inspiration for the words. Here I found that Blake had, allegedly, based *Jerusalem* on a well-known story, which suggests that Joseph of Arimathea took Jesus on a trip to Albion or Ancient Britain to be tutored by its wise Druids. [2] When I re-read the words from *Jerusalem*, I could see just why the conspiracy theorists had come up with this idea:

And did those feet in ancient time
Walk upon England's mountains Green?
And was the holy Lamb of God
On pleasant pastures seen?

After contacting the British Library about this issue, I was provided with a link to a strange engraving that had been produced by Blake, which was held at the Morgan Library and Museum, in New York.[3] It depicts Joseph of Arimathea standing on the rocks of Albion (fig. 32).

From Blake to the Word

While rooting through the many strands of this mystery, I found that William Blake had produced a handful of strange 'prophetic' works about Ancient Albion and its earliest native Druids. These works were eventually adopted by various esoteric movements,[4] such as the Hermetic Order of the Golden Dawn, which flourished in the late 19th and early 20th centuries. As well

Figure 32

as Blake's prophetic works, the Golden Dawn used the same manuscripts as the Hermetic Rosicrucians to form its ritualistic practices, such as the *Book of Enoch* and the *Key of Solomon*.[5] Not to mention that one of its founding members, Dr. William Wynn Westcott, was an active member of the *Societas Rosicruciana in Anglia*, or 'Rosicrucian Order in England'[6]; the relevance of which will become apparent in the next degree.

Blake also produced another work using the title *Jerusalem*. In this, his last epic work, he suggested that Jerusalem in the Holy Land was an emanation or product of Ancient Albion. In other words, he believed that Ancient Albion was the original Jerusalem. Adding to this revolutionary idea, just like in the Enoch legend, he also suggested that the Albion Druids had passed on their knowledge to early cultures from the East. Blake put forward the following words to summarise his provocative ideas:

Jerusalem the Emanation of the Giant Albion! Can it be? Is it a Truth that the Learned [Albion Druids] have explored? Was Britain the Primitive Seat of the Patriarchal Religion? All things Begin & End in Albion's Ancient Druid Rocky Shore...[7]

Blake also composed his epic *Jerusalem* to explain to the contemporary cultures in the East that the Druids had taught their ancestors a very specific tradition:

You have a tradition that Man anciently contained in his mighty limbs all things in Heaven & Earth: this you received from the Druids.[8]

For me, these words were describing the concept of intelligent design or the Philosophers' Stone; the idea that we, as humans, hold in us the very essence of God's creative expression – His secret knowledge. Blake produced many drawings to illustrate his *Jerusalem*; and when I eventually tracked them down, I found myself staring in amazement at his final, 100th drawing, depicting the stylised Great Architect with his divider (fig. 33), standing before some sort of Druid temple or henge.[9] The next day I took a copy of the engraving to George.

"Do you get it?" he asked, tracing over the henge with his finger. "What is the Grand Architect trying to show us?"

Figure 33

"I see it; the Grand Architect is showing us that his geometric, secret knowledge can be found within the proportions of the temple."

"That's right, the secret in us is the proportions of the temple, the blueprint; the temple that provides the gateway to Paradise. Both Blake and Isaac Newton were well aware of this fact."

"Isaac Newton?"

"Yes, he also discovered the blueprint."

Solomon's Temple and the Word

I soon discovered that Blake was intrigued by Isaac Newton, the English physicist, mathematician, astronomer, natural philosopher and alchemist. As you can see (fig. 34), he produced a strange drawing of Newton, depicting him as some sort of Great Architect, using his divider to check certain geometric proportions, similar to those of the Philosophers' Stone.[10]

While looking into Blake's inspiration for this drawing, I found that, as with many other members of

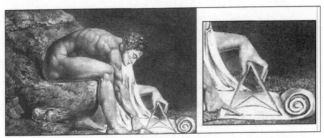

Figure 34

The Royal Society, Newton had been accused of being a Rosicrucian.[11] I also found that he studied and wrote extensively about Solomon's Temple.[12] Just like the story surrounding the nature of Solomon's keyword, Newton believed that King Solomon had hidden a complex code of symbolic and mathematical language into the temple's architecture, which, when deciphered, would reveal a divine blueprint.[13]

In one of Newton's more obscure works, *The Chronology of Ancient Kingdoms*, he went to great lengths to document the proportions of Solomon's Temple. Having acquired a copy of the work, I saw that his first words centred on the orientation of the temple, in that it was set-out to the east. I also found other important snippets of information along the way, but as I reached the end of his work, it suddenly came to me that I had omitted to pursue an obvious line of enquiry; I had not taken the time to study Solomon's Temple.

As part of my new enquiry, I discovered that it was from the site of Solomon's Temple that prophet Mohamed had travelled up a ladder of light to meet with Allah and see the delights of Paradise.[14] Moreover, within the Bible I discovered that the holiest place in the temple, the Holy of Holies, had been built to act as a link or nexus between heaven and earth, which was hidden behind a veil containing three colours: blue to represent heaven, red to represent earth, and purple to represent the meeting of the celestial and terrestrial worlds.[15] But what really blew me away was the episode in the Bible where God appeared to offer Solomon his Word, so that he could build the temple:

> ...the Lord came to Solomon saying: Concerning this temple which you are building, if you walk in My statutes, execute My judgement, keep all My commandments, and walk in them, then I will perform my Word with you.[16]

Even though I had recently talked to George, I felt that I had no option but to ask for guidance, so made my way back to the shop. As per usual he quickly moved the conversation in a new and novel direction.

"This episode you've found in the Bible that talks about the Lost Word and the temple is obviously part of the hidden Gnostic story. This being the case, we cannot be sure which god wanted to give Solomon the Word."

"What do you mean, which god?"

"If I were to hazard a guess, it would have to be Sabaoth, the same one who gave Solomon the ring so that he could direct the demonic-Genii to help build his temple."

"So you think that, as part of the master plan, Sabaoth was sent to help Solomon build the temple?"

"No, to build a temple to hide the Word, for the prophesised adepts to find."

"So can we really build a temple to access Paradise, or is it just an ancient, esoteric concept?"

"Well, only you can decide that, but as I have already told you, the temple has been built and it now resides within Blake's Jerusalem."

"So the temple is located where?"

"You can walk to it from your house."

Taken aback, I began racking my brains to find a temple in York that fitted the bill, but nothing was forthcoming.

"Come on George, give me a break."

"Well, what I will tell you is that the temple sits on the symbolic site where the first Christian Roman emperor was crowned; the epicentre of the original Jerusalem, Eborakon."

8ᵗʰ Degree

The Ogdoad House of Anu

It was on the evening of March 20, 2004, when I typed the words "first Christian Roman Emperor crowned York" into a search engine. Immediately I got a hit, which explained that in the year 306 Constantine was crowned at Eboracum, Ebor, present day York. In fact, the Holy Roman Emperor can still be found today sitting proudly outside York Minster (fig. 35).

Figure 35

When I read about Constantine's coronation on the now site of York Minster, a vivid image of the immense Gothic building flashed before my eyes. I immediately purged it from my mind, not believing that it could have anything to do with the site of the original Jerusalem and the quest to regain Paradise. But I could hear a voice urging me to follow the mystery, to follow the White Rabbit, to follow the clues left by the medieval artisans. It was in this moment that I saw the inevitability of my destiny.

Minster Masons and the Tree of Life

Even though my heart was telling me to just go down to the Minster and start looking for clues, I decided instead to go with my head and visit the York Minster Library.

As a starting point I began researching the design of the Minster, to see if I could find anything of interest in its architecture. Initially, I discovered that it was east-facing, and that it had been constructed to represent a crucifix. As you can see with the plan of the Minster (fig. 36), there is also an octagonal temple attached to its north side, which is generally referred to as the Chapter House.

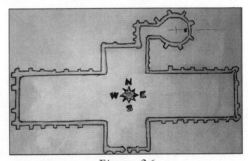

Figure 36

On the third morning of entering the Minster Library, as per usual, I passed through its large oak door, approached the counter and signed in. A stern-looking, middle-aged man immediately caught my eye and beckoned me over.

"I hope you don't mind, but one of the librarians mentioned that you had been looking for evidence of anything occult in the architecture of the Minster. Is there anything that I can help you with?"

"Well, truth be known, I don't quite know what I'm looking for, but I think I'll know when I find it."

The man must have enjoyed my response because he laughed out loud.

"Well if you don't find what you don't know what you're looking for, give me a shout."

He rushed by me and disappeared up a large, stone staircase. As I stood there listening to his steps fade into an inaudible thump, I realised that I had missed out on a golden opportunity, so I turned and headed up the stairs after him. When I reached the top and entered the silent reading room, I saw that he had slipped into a glass-encased office. Not wanting to break the silence, I carefully made my way over and raised my hand to the glass, giving him a vibrant smile. He beckoned me in and offered me a seat, which I took.

"So how can I help?"

As the question and answer session progressed, I believe I caught his imagination, and he soon after began scribbling frantically on a large yellow Post-it note, while tapping what I assumed were search enquiries into the library's database. After a few minutes watching him at work, he peeled away the top leaf of the pad and offered it to me.

"These references will certainly help, and do please be sure to let me know if you find anything 'esoteric'. Actually, just give me a moment."

He stood up, took down an old book from a shelf and began flicking through it. As he turned over the pages, I noticed several engravings of what I assumed were depictions of the internal architecture of the Minster.

When he eventually found the engraving he was looking for, he turned the book round.

"As you can see from the date, this plate shows the Armorial Window; a mysterious stained glass window that was placed in the Minster just after its construction, in the 13th century. This plate was engraved in 1736 by a man named Francis Drake, who was once the Masonic Grand Master of the Grand Lodge of All England, at York.[1] He was the one who produced the epic work about the history of York; he called it Eboracum or Ebor for short. This might be a good place to start."

Inspired by the engraving, the next morning I took the leap and made my way down to York's illustrious, solemn temple. When I entered the Minster I headed straight for the 'Masonic' window. Instead of being captivated by the intricacy of the stained glass artwork, I found myself staring at the stone inscription at its base (fig. 37).

Figure 37

After several minutes observing the Masonic divider and reference to the Great Architect of the Universe, I had a little scout-round to see if I could find anything else of interest. To my amazement, I discovered a small Masonic chapel just across from the window, which not only held in its ironwork the divider, but also the all-seeing eye of God at the centre of Solomon's Temple Seal. The same seal adopted by the Jewish Nation as its symbol (fig. 38).

When I got back home I turned to my computer and typed in 'Ebor Ebocarum', in an attempt to locate some

Figure 38

information about the nature of the Grand Master's work; and it was here that I found something quite unique.

Many people believe that the place-name Ebor or Eboracum was applied to the now York by the Romans. In truth, before the Romans arrived, the place was actually called Eborakon. For instance, in Ptolemy's so-called *Geography* of the 2nd century AD, Eborakon is listed as one of the towns attributed to the druidical Brigante tribe; *akon* meaning 'place of' and *Ebor* (taken from the word *Eburos*) meaning 'Yew tree'.[2] Hence, York was originally known as 'The Place of the Yew Tree'. This seemingly obscure fact started me thinking about the druidical, life-giving mythology associated with the yew tree Yggdrasil, the Tree of Life. I even started to visualise Enoch again, this time alongside the Druids in the North, tutoring him about the fragrant tree's immortalising properties. It then came to me that Eborakon, in druidical terms, would be best described not as the Place of the Yew Tree, but as the Place of the Tree of Life.

Whilst visiting George to share my mysterious findings, I was hopeful that he would explain a little of their significance. To my delight, when I had just about finished revealing everything, he tapped his temple three times.

"Oh, this is just the tip of the iceberg, the Minster holds unimaginable secrets."

"Secrets?"

"The site of the Minster in *Eborakon*, the 'Place of the Yew Tree', the original Jerusalem, was the ancient centre for Druid worship."

He then changed tact and began talking about something called the Ancient Druid Order, but before he could get into any detail the Saturday morning rush hit the shop. So I gave my usual thanks, indicated that I would phone him and headed for the door. However, just before I disappeared, George called out over the cacophony of voices.

"Godfrey Higgins I presume."

"Godfrey Higgins?"

"Yes, Godfrey will lead you to the gateway."

After a good week of research, I found that Godfrey Higgins was born in 1772 at Skellow Grange, Yorkshire, close to where I was born; and that throughout his life he had been many things, including, a Fellow of the Society of Antiquaries, Major in the British Army and one of the most important Freemasons in England.[3] After leaving the army, Higgins dedicated his life to solving some of the deepest mysteries known to humankind, and in due course his extensive knowledge led to his appointment as Chosen Chief of the Ancient Druid Order.[4]

As Chosen Chief, Higgins produced an extensive work on the nature of the British Druids, entitled *Celtic Druids*, which basically expands on the concept put forward by William Blake; in that the Druids were responsible for influencing early cultures in the East. I also found that Godfrey Higgins had succeeded William Blake as Chosen Chief of the Ancient Druid Order,[5] which explained a lot. But what intrigued me most about Higgins was that he had produced documents about an early Rosicrucian group in York, which had performed its rituals inside York Minster. How I came across this obscure fact is quite long winded, but in short, I was told by a professor of Freemasonry when I visited a centre dedicated to research into the art of Freemasonry. On the afternoon I entered the professor's office, I could tell straight away that he was curious about my interest in Higgins, because he shook my hand vigorously and smiled profusely as he offered me a seat.

"So you're trying to rediscover one of the most obscure yet influential characters from the recesses of Masonic history?"

"Yes, it seems to me that Higgins had his fingers in more than the Masonic pie."

He sat down and tapped out a short beat on the surface of his desk.

"I suppose we had better get down to business then. I have done a little work on Higgins myself and I think this will be a good place to start."

He took out a wad of paper from the bottom drawer of his desk.

"The latest part of the puzzle surrounding Higgins was recently discovered in the Library and Museum of Freemasonry."

"Puzzle?"

"Yes, puzzle. It seems that Higgins had access to all areas; and this recently discovered letter tells us all about his powerful connections. It talks about his absence from a special Grand Masonic Feast."

"Absence from a feast?"

"Yes, absence. He could not attend the feast because he had been in York, searching into the antiquities of Masonry by the desire of his Royal Highness, the Duke of Sussex." [6]

"Now that's really interesting. York you say?"

"It was in York that Higgins made contact with the last surviving member of a Rosicrucian group that..."

"Rosicrucian group."

"Yes, a Rosicrucian group that conducted its business inside the Minster."

"What, York Minster?"

"Look here, Higgins describes the group as a Druidical Lodge or encampment." [7] If you take the time to read through this document, you will see that Higgins' research into the Minster-based Rosicrucian group enchanted several other prominent freemasons, including the hermetic scholar William Wynn Westcott." [8]

"Yes, I know of Westcott, he was a member of the English Rosicrucian Order, the founding member of the Hermetic Order of the Golden Dawn. He championed Blake's ideas about the influence of the Albion Druids on early cultures from the East."

Looking surprised by my diverse knowledge, the professor took hold of his chin.

"Westcott's curiosity about the Minster-based group would have been well-founded, especially if it was as old as Higgins had suspected."

I could see that he was waiting for my response to his thought-provoking statement. "Maybe Westcott believed that the Rosicrucian group held information from the time of Francis Bacon."

Seeing that he was unmoved by this proposition, I decided to take it a little further.

"Maybe Westcott was looking to unlock God's secret knowledge. Maybe he was looking for the same thing as Francis Bacon's College of the Six Dayes Workes in *New Atlantis*; the Philosophers' Stone, the keyword, the Lost Word of God."

Glaring at me with one eye closed, the professor leaned forward and scribbled down a name on the wad of paper.

"Just ask one of the York Minster Police and you will be sure to get hold of this guy, I am sure that he will be able to help."

A day or so after this enlightening conversation, and with George's words echoing in my mind, I visited the Minster again to see if I could find the professor's contact. As it turned out, he was a member of the Minster Police, and it took little over ten minutes to locate him.

The Minster guide who pointed me in his direction explained that he was dealing with a suspected broken leg on the steps of the Minster. After watching a poor old woman being loaded into an ambulance, I approached the policeman.

"I know this is not the best time, but could you possibly help me with my search for the Minster's Rosicrucians?"

"Why don't we take a little walk around this ancient pile of stone?"

He casually brushed down his sandstone-marked knees.

"I suppose you would like to know about the secret room in the Minster, where the Rosicrucians performed their most profound rituals?"

"Yes, if you don't mind," I replied, as we slowly moved away from the entrance.

"Well, we don't know when the Rosicrucians began using it, but we do know that it was taken over by the Masonic Grand Lodge of all England in the latter part of the 1700s."

"So is it possible to see the room?"

"Well, you will first have to acquire special permission."

After observing the full extent of the disappointment on my face he smiled.

"But what the hell, rules are made for breaking."

"Could we get into trouble?"

"Don't act daft lad, we can do anything, I'm the Chief of Police."

I returned to the Minster just before its ancient doors were closed for the night. As I made my way inside, I immediately came face-to-face with the Chief, who placed a finger on his lips and nodded twice to indicate that we were on a covert mission.

He pushed a large key into the Minster door's iron lock, turned it, and with this the Minster was ours. He then led me towards the north side of the immense Gothic structure, until we arrived at the east-facing corridor that links to its octagonal temple, the Chapter House. Half way down the corridor he stopped and pointed to the ceiling, which I could just about make out in the shadows.

"It's above us."

The hairs on the back of my neck stood up, and we proceeded to enter into the Chapter House. Once we had passed through into the massive octagonal temple, the Chief took hold of its large wooden doors and began pushing them, until the dim light from the corridor was no more. In the darkness I heard what sounded like a switch click, and then a slither of light appeared on the floor, casting long shadows from his boots. After a moment or two I heard his keys rattle, and then the unmistakable scrape of an old mortise lock.

"We've only got five minutes," he suddenly uttered, as he slowly opened a small door to reveal a spiral staircase.

Half way up the staircase the Chief stopped.

"We are about to enter into a room that not only acted as a secret retreat for the Rosicrucians, but also as the tracing board floor for the master stonemason to draw out his geometric plans for the special window supports in the Chapter House."

We then swirled around the last level of the staircase, and with my heart racing we entered the secret room. I must admit, I was a little disappointed with what I saw, but nevertheless I slipped out my camera, turned it on and grabbed the money shot (fig. 39). When the flash went off the Chief was not impressed, but I apologised profusely.

Figure 39

After looking around the sparse interior, and observing the intricate geometric shapes, which the master stonemason had carved into the floor several hundred years before, the Chief informed me that it was time to go. So I thanked him for the experience and we retraced our steps back to the Minster's entrance. Here I gave my final thanks and headed down the steps towards the bronze figure of the Holy Roman Emperor. Just before I reached the patina-stained statue, I heard him call out.

"The Rosicrucians also used the Chapter House for their rituals."

Having already decided that I would be paying another visit to the octagonal temple, I simply turned, tapped my temple and set-off for the kebab van that was usually parked-up next to Whipmawhopmagate.

The Gateway to the House of Anu

On the following Sunday morning I eagerly made my way back to the Minster and headed straight for the Chapter House. As I made my way inside I saw that it was full of tourists. I also noticed that its doors had been pushed back into place, hiding the entrance to the Rosicrucian room. Unsure what to do next, I began working my way around the interior of the octagonal structure, while at the same time examining the ornate carvings of the Messiah, grotesques, angels and mythical animals. After a minute or so I found myself standing next to a Minster guide that had accidentally bumped into me.

I purposefully caught her eye and then looked down to her name badge.

"Excuse me Lily, could I possibly talk to you about the Chapter House?"

"Of course, what do you want to know?"

"Well, for instance, who is that stone figure behind you, and why is he there?"

"Ah, Shin, the Toothache Man, has baffled many a scholar. In fact, all of the Chapter House's weird Pagan icons are for some reason still intact. They escaped the frenzied practice of iconoclasm in the time of Protestant Reformation."

"Iconoclasm?"

"Yes, the act of image-breaking. I suppose the Chapter House was not vandalised by the purists because someone must have deemed it too important to deface."

"Important you say? I suppose this leads me nicely to my next question. You wouldn't by any chance know about the Rosicrucian's interest in the Chapter House?"

She looked at her watch.

"Sorry, I really have to go now."

Before she turned to leave, an obscure question suddenly popped into my mind.

"So why is the Chapter House shaped like an octagon?"

She laughed.

"I assume it has something to do with the Ogdoad."

"Ogdoad?"

Unfortunately she was well on the way to the Chapter House's doors, and simply turned and smiled as she disappeared down the corridor that sits underneath the Rosicrucian room. This was not the last of Lily.

Curious about the word Ogdoad, when I got back home I typed it into a search engine and soon discovered that it had been used by many cultures to describe a religious idea. What really caught my imagination was that the early Egyptian-Gnostics and later Hermetic Rosicrucians used the word "Ogdoad" to describe the celestial realm of the gods; the eight-fold realm, the eighth heaven, or Paradise if you like.[9]

To gain more insight into this ancient idea, I made contact with the School of Culture and Communication at the University of Melbourne. Based on the department's involvement with the study of Christian iconography, I assumed it would be a good place to start; and I was not wrong, since the doctor who responded to my enquiry had much insight into the nature of the Ogdoad, as outlined in her email:

Hi there Richard. The Christian interpretation of the octagonal or Ogdoad form is rooted in very old traditions. It most likely arcs back to the idea of eternal salvation or immortality. In fact, the eight-fold system in the East was similarly employed in the design of temples, the Taoist's Eight Immortals Temple being one such example. It also extends to the trigrams of I Ching, and can be found in the design of Islamic and pre-Islamic temples. In Cyril Glasse, *The New Enciclopedia of Islam*, p. 122, it states that the temple-octagon is a step in the mathematical series; from square (symbolising earth), to circle (symbolising heaven). In many respects the universal dome-covered octagon that appears in Christian settings is attuned to the ancient idea that the temple is a celestial conduit, a link between this world and the immortal realm. For example, in many Saints' tombs the base forms the square or four corners of the earth in the octagonal structure, and the topping dome represents the circle of heaven. This configuration again depicts the idea of a celestial, terrestrial link. But I would say that the influence of the octagonal form most likely arcs back to the Ogdoad realm in the Egyptian belief system. Hope all this helps.

While focussing on the idea that the dome-covered Ogdoad-temple represented a link between heaven and earth, I found that it had been used in many diverse settings. For instance, a massive dome atop an octagonal structure exists not only at the heart of St. Paul's Cathedral in London, but also at the Dome of the Rock, which now covers the once Holy of Holies at Solomon's Temple; the same place from which Mohammed made his trip to heaven. But what really got me thinking, after studying an old drawing of the Chapter House, was that it too employed this ancient geometric concept (fig. 40). [10] For instance, on the right is the old etching of the Chapter House's domed roof and on the left an overall plan of its Ogdoad or octagonal structure.

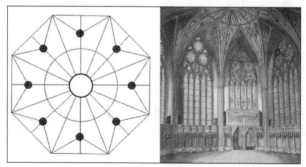

Figure 40

It was at this point that I started to appreciate the importance of the Ogdoad in temple design. It was undoubtedly employed to 'geometrically attune' the temple to the eight-fold realm, to the home of the gods, defining the metaphorical nexus between earth and heaven; an idea that was at the heart of the quest to regain Paradise. As I continued to work on this idea, I began thinking about the earliest depiction of the gateway to the home of the gods, the House of Anu, where the Cherubins or Tammuz and Gishzida were guarding the Tree of Life (fig 11).

Figure 11

At the time, it seemed that the geometric expression of the Ogdoad was far removed from this ancient, pictorial vision of the celestial abode, but something was telling me that there had to be a connection, which I was obviously missing. I even had a vivid dream that gave me a poetical way in which to merge these two seemingly disparate concepts together, which began in the corridor leading to the Chapter House. Here the White Rabbit and policeman were beckoning me to kneel before its large wooden doors, to pay homage to the guardians of the Tree of Life at the entrance to the Ogdoad realm. Of course, this was just a weird dream, but it did inspire me to revisit the Minster Library, to see if I could find any evidence of the Tree of Life in the Chapter House's architecture.

On entering the library, I made my way upstairs to see my new 'esoteric' friend. To my delight he was sitting where I had left him.

"Now that's weird," he said, as I entered the office. "Just last night I was talking to the theologian for the Minster, telling him about your ideas. Have you made any progress?"

"Well, I have in a way, but I am now after something very specific."

"Fire away. I am all ears."

"Well it's really quite simple; is there anything in the architecture of the Chapter House that relates to the Tree of Life?"

"Let's see. Not in the windows. Not in the carvings. Ah, now that's a thought."

He picked up his pen and pressed it onto his nose.

"Does a Tree of Life made out of metal count?"

"Even spaghetti would do."

"Spaghetti, that would go nicely with a bottle of Italian red. I can almost taste it."

"I get your drift. But seriously, it's important, is there a representation of the Tree of Life in the Chapter House."

"Well, after I had told the theologian all about our conversation, he mentioned the Tree of Life on the Chapter House's doors. He explained that it was there to signify the entrance to God's house. He also said something about the Tree of Life being reserved in Paradise for the so-called souls of the pure, at the End of Days."

"That's good. That's really good."

"Well, I'm glad to help again. I hope you will keep me posted."

That evening I re-entered the Chapter House with a new sense of excitement. I was surprised to find it empty of tourists. Without delay I took hold of its massive doors, pulled them back towards the corridor and stepped away. As my eyes began to make sense of what stood before me, my heart began to race again. At first I saw the swirling metal forms that had been attached to the doors, which were sprouting from a central support. A wave of emotion began to take hold of me, my dream was coming true, there was an ornate representation of the Tree of Life covering the Chapter House's doors. Frantically, I began searching for its guardians, moving my eyes gradually upwards, following each bud-laden swirl to its centre. As I reached the *eighth* and final piece of scrolled ironmongery, I saw them, inconspicuously hidden at the pinnacle of the tree (fig. 41). It was the griffin-type creatures, Tammuz and Gishzida, guarding the Tree of Life at the gateway to Paradise.

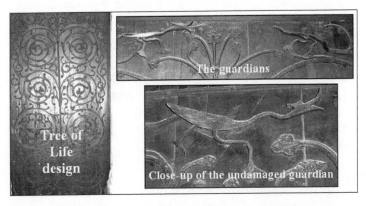

Figure 41

Whilst describing to George on the phone what I had discovered, I could hear him moving around, and then the unmistakable sliding of the glass from the cabinet at the back of the shop.

"So what do you think then George?"

"Well, I think it is now time to delve into the prophesy."

I could hear him whispering, most likely reading from a text that he had removed from the cabinet.

"What is it?"

"One moment."

I heard a page turn.

"Here we are. The White Rabbit not only denotes the key in us, but also the Venus-prophesy; the prophesy that is reserved solely for the prophesised adepts."

I was baffled by his strange words, but then it suddenly dawned on me; I sort of knew what he was talking about.

"That's right. Venus was depicted by several ancient cultures as the White Rabbit."

George cleared his throat.

"Now a great sign appeared in the heavens, a woman, clothed with the sun on her final transit. Wait. If the Venus prophesy from the *Book of Revelation* can be unravelled, Mohamed will smile from the eighth heaven in hope."

"Mohamed? From the *Book of Revelation*?"

"Yes, Revelation, the disclosure of secrets to man, by the Divine."

"So what does this mean?"

"It means that the *Book of Revelation* holds the revelation, all you have to do is decode it."

9th Degree

The Venus Prophesy

To get to grips with the idea that the White Rabbit symbolised not only the key for unlocking God's secret knowledge in us, but also some sort of Venus-prophesy, I first took out the stepladders and made my way up into the loft. As I lifted the top off an old storage box, labelled '1989/90', I came face to face with my missing copy of the 1611 *King James' Bible*, alongside the mystical images that had started me on my mysterious journey.

Figure 1

Venus

While reading through my old notes, I came across the description of Mohamed's 'vision' of Venus and the crescent moon. I could not help but think that this archaic, celestial symbolism would somehow help me to discover

the Venus-prophesy; symbolism that had been adopted b.
Islam from its conception.

I then turned to the *Book of Revelation*, but found
it hard going, since it was littered with what I can only
describe as Gnostic-speak. So I decided to change tact and
began looking into the mythology surrounding Venus.
This way I knew that I would be better equipped to
identify any cryptic references to the planet, assuming that
any existed in the *Book of Revelation*.

I was initially drawn to the planet's well-known
association with the pentacle and rose, since it was also
astronomical in nature. For instance, Venus traces out a
pentacle or rose shape in the heavens over an *eight* year
period; which is an event that features prominently in the
teachings of various occult fraternities, including those of
the Rose Cross or Rosicrucian Order.[1] However, it was
a few days later, while holding a copy of *Wayne's World*
and a curry in the local DVD store when things got really
interesting.

An old, tramp-like gentleman that was stood just
behind me was shouting across to an assistant, asking for
advice about a film.

"This film, *Revelation*, is it worth watching?"

"Well, it's quite an interesting one really," the assistant
explained. "It's about occult symbols and the race to find
a sacred object."

"Sacred object?" I interjected. Strangely, the old man
winked at me. I winked back and smiled. He laughed and
headed for the door. I felt that something was not quite
right.

"Yes, I believe it's based on the *Book of Revelation*
from the Bible and something to do with the planet
Venus," the assistant continued.

I checked to see if I was dreaming. It all seemed just a little too strange that I should be talking to an assistant in a DVD store about Venus and *Revelation*. Nevertheless, when I reached the front of the queue, I passed over *Wayne's World* and pointed over to the rental section.

"Do you have a copy of that *Revelation* film to buy?"

"Yes. If you plump for the buy one get one free deal," the assistant replied, with an American twang, "*Wayne's World* and *Revelation* will only cost you 8.99."

"Great, I'll take the deal."

When I arrived back home with my diverse acquisitions, I cracked the curry and a bottle of red, unwrapped *Revelation* and placed it into the DVD player. Straight away, the nature of the sacred relic in the film, the *Loculus* or 'key', was revealed. If you haven't seen the film I don't want to spoil it, but in short the means by which to break the 'code' of the Loculus sits with the symbols that are carved into a wooden box by a sect of early Gnostics; namely, the caduceus and the Anch, both the feminine symbol for Venus and the Egyptian symbol for the Tree of Life. As part of the film, when the Anch is overlaid on a map of Europe, it points to the location of a Venus temple, on the island of Patmos; the same island on which the *Book of Revelation* was written by John the Divine. Stuart Urbine (the writer and director of the film) also has it that the true power of the Loculus can only be unleashed when Venus is in the 'perfect position in the heavens'.

Realising the significance of this, I decided to make contact with Stuart and emailed him through his production company, Cyclops Vision, to see if he knew anything about the Venus prophesy in the *Book of*

Revelation. To my delight I received a response the next day:

Thanks for all that. It's all fascinating stuff isn't it? Similar ideas are contained in the film, but there's also some interesting stuff in the special features section of the DVD. I suggest you run your prophetic idea by one of the gents starring in the DVD's special features section, he's a specialist in the religious occult. The *Book of Revelation* has been interpreted in many ways over the years and it is undoubtedly based around the forthcoming salvation of the human race. You will have noticed that this idea is referred to as *Palingenisis* in the film, which, in the Gospel of Matthew, Jesus uses to describe the Last Judgement, but it also translates to 'rebirth'. I suppose this all ties in with your novel idea about the quest to regain salvation or Paradise... Venus as the Anch etc. Below is the phone number... we wish you good luck with your quest...

Intrigued by what the DVD special features gent might have to say, I picked up the phone and gave him a ring. After explaining how I had acquired his number, I quickly got down to business.

"So, basically, I would really like to know if there is a Venus-prophesy hidden within the *Book of Revelation*."

"Ah, the sun clothed woman."

Instantly the words that George had spoken from his mysterious source came to mind and I said them out loud.

"A great sign appeared in the heavens, a woman clothed with the sun."

"That's right, the sun clothed woman, Venus. She denotes the astronomical circumstances surrounding the timing of *Revelation*."

"Astronomical circumstances. Timing. Do you mean timing as in a prophetic event?"

"Yes, when the sun clothed woman or Venus passes the sun, the road to salvation will be revealed."

"Passes the sun?"

"I believe this is known in astronomical terms as the transit of Venus. Only very rarely does she transit the sun, but if it were possible to work out which transit the *Book of Revelation* is describing, then we would know the start date of the events that appear in John's vision."

"Look, do you mind if I contact you again at a later date? I really need to get my head around this transit thing."

"No bother. It's an interesting subject and I'm always on the lookout for new and novel theories for my books. If you do find anything be sure to let me know."

After putting the telephone down, I took out my Bible and turned again to the *Book of Revelation*. I also connected to the internet and typed in the words "Venus transit sun". Clicking on the hits, whilst reading about John the Divine's vision, I noticed that someone had taken the time to illustrate the connection between the sun clothed woman in the *Book of Revelation* and Venus' rare transit across the sun (fig. 42). [2]

After a few minutes skim-reading through the biblical work, I came to the lines that describe this symbolic event:

A great and wondrous sign appeared in the heaven: a woman [Venus] clothed with the sun, with the moon under her feet...[3]

Figure 42

Realising that the sun clothed woman (Venus) was standing on the moon, it seemed to me that John was not just referring to her transit, but also to the prophetic symbol adopted by the Islamic Faith, the coming-together of Venus and the crescent moon. I turned back to the images on my computer screen and noticed that the sun clothed woman was indeed standing on the crescent moon. I promptly printed the images out and placed them alongside the images from my early research (fig. 43).

Figure 43

While thinking about the duel-symbolic meaning of the White Rabbit and Venus, as part of the quest to regain Paradise, I turned to the window, closed my eyes and let the heat of the low sun pound down on my face. Having stared at the blinding light momentarily before closing my eyes, I could see a residual image of a white disc surrounded by blackness. As a cloud passed by and the window cracked I received a revelation; I had no option but to try and work out just when the prophetic events in the *Book of Revelation* would take place.

I turned again to my computer and typed in "timing transit of Venus". Clicking on the link to the NASA site dedicated to this event,[4] described as "one of the rarest of planetary alignments with the sun", I found that two transits were due to take place in this century; the first being now, in 2004, and the second in 2012.

To see if these dates had any significance, I proceeded to type them into the computer, but found nothing of interest about the year 2004. However, when I typed in 2012, I was literally flabbergasted by what came up.

Of course, the hype surrounding the astronomical prophesies or so-called 2012 phenomenon has now passed, and the world still remains. But at the time, with very little written about this date, I was intrigued to find that it had been revered by ancient cultures and prominent individuals throughout the ages. It was certainly a line of enquiry that could not be dismissed.

After a couple of days rooting through the extent of the 2012 phenomenon, I found that the transit of Venus was just one part of a much larger prophetic-astronomical spectacular. For instance, not long after 2012 the sun will rise directly in front of the Galactic equator, signifying the beginning of the end of an ancient, astronomical cycle. I also found that there was much debate surrounding this 2012 phenomenon, which was split between two possible outcomes. The first being the destruction of all life on earth, and the second being a secret dawning of a new age that would lead to our physical and spiritual transformation; a transformation that would ultimately result in a collective-human actualisation, enabling us to restore Paradise here on earth.[5]

I turned again to the *Book of Revelation*, to see what would happen to the human race once this prophetic event had come to fruition. When I read what John the Divine had been told about this issue, I nearly fell off my chair:

> To him who overcomes I will give to eat of the Tree of Life, which is in the Paradise of my God.[6]

Realising the immense significance of this to the quest to regain Paradise, I continued to read and was similarly shocked when I found what would happen to the one responsible for restoring Paradise on earth:

> He who overcomes, I will make him a pillar in the temple of my God...I will write on him the name of my God, and the name of the city of my God, the New Jerusalem.[7]

When I took all this to George I was expecting him to congratulate me on a job well done. Instead, he simply stood up, put on his coat and began explaining about the prophesy.

"I have no doubt that in 2012 someone will be standing at the gateway in New Jerusalem, the same site as the original Jerusalem, Eborakon. But they will only begin the fight for the Tree of Life. They will not complete it."

"Begin the fight? What, in the Chapter House? Are you saying that I will have to be in the Chapter House in 2012? What day in 2012?"

"The date is, traditionally, December 21, 2012, the Winter Solstice, the end date of the Mesoamerican Long Count calendar, but this is not the end, just the secret beginning of the end. Certain things have to be found if the final adepts are to take their rightful place."

"Like what?"

"I do believe that the symbolic ode left to Godfrey Higgins, the Chief Druid, will bring clarity to your thoughts. Come on, I'll shut up shop and take you to see his legacy."

Godfrey Higgins and Venus

It was around mid-afternoon when George and I arrived at Red House Business Park, which is situated on the high ground looking-out over Skellow Grange, where Godfrey Higgins once resided. After parking at the bottom of the complex we set off up the hill, until we had a panoramic view of the Skellow landscape.

We stood there for a few moments until George broke the silence.

"Do you see it?"

Not wanting to disappoint him, I carefully surveyed the greenery for a few moments more, but saw nothing out of the ordinary.

"No, sorry, I just can't see…"

Before I had finished the sentence my eyes met with something very familiar in the distance, a gigantic crescent moon (fig. 44).

Figure 44

"So what about the silver planet, Venus?" asked George.

Luckily I was ahead of him this time and saw her, just beneath us (fig. 45).

Figure 45

"So are you saying that this is somehow a tribute to Godfrey's knowledge of the prophetic events from the *Book of Revelation* and the quest to regain Paradise?"

Instead of responding, George turned and headed up the hill, towards the top of the complex. I too turned and made my way up the hill. When I eventually caught up with him, I saw that he was standing at the centre of a large metal arrangement, which had been cast to incorporate the crescent moon and Venus pairing (fig. 46).

Figure 46

To gain a better view, I scrambled-up towards the highest ground. When I reached the top, I realised just what it was; a metal representation of an early druidical henge, just like Uriel's Machine and the henges at Thornborough (fig. 47).

Figure 47

After several minutes scrutinising the familiar arrangement, I found myself staring at two flags that were

Figure 48

flying in the grounds of one of the nearby warehouses; one containing an orange and white corporate identity and the other an image of the anchor-symbol (fig.48).

Captivated by the imagery, I began thinking about the relationship between Venus and the crescent moon, and for the first time I sort of understood what the early Gnostic Christians were attempting to portray with their secret symbol. For me, the Anch resting in a curved vessel was representative of Venus standing on the crescent moon; a Gnostic symbol that represented Hope in the form of salvation (fig.49). It was the symbol at the heart of the *Book of Revelation*, the book describing the disclosure of secrets to man, by the Divine.

Figure 49

As I began to play with this idea, various images started to flash through my mind and many seemingly random connections began fusing together in an instance, until, finally, the extent of the prophesy appeared as a revelation before my eyes (fig. 50).

Figure 50

What I found most satisfying was that I had worked out just why the Rosicrucian Master, Francis Bacon, had placed the snake-entwined anchor on the title page of his work, *New Atlantis*. This work was dedicated to a Rosicrucian college striving to unlock God's secret knowledge in us; the same knowledge that would allow us to not only build a temple to access the celestial realm, but also gain access to the Tree of Life and ultimately regain our Paradise. When I made my way back down to George and told him about my revelation, he nodded slowly.

"The coming-together of Venus and the crescent moon is indeed an archaic expression that has been hidden within the inner recesses of the human psyche from the beginning. They will come together twice in 2012. You are now aware that this symbol is not only the symbol of Hope, but also the astronomical symbol that denotes the time when the last leg of the quest to regain Paradise will begin."

"The same time when Venus is clothed with the sun?"

"Yes, in 2012. But the temple gateway still has to be discovered."

"Discovered?"

"Yes, discovered. And there is one more thing to do before you can seek out the gateway; you must unravel the artisans' mystery system, the backbone of their secret story, which appears in the misericord carvings. It was also hidden within the teachings of Speculative Freemasonry to ensure its survival through the ages."

"The artisans' mystery system, the secret story, can also be found in the Freemasonry teachings? I think I know the right man to contact about this."

10th Degree

Order of the Rose

In an attempt to unravel the artisans' mystery system, I contacted the professor from the centre dedicated to research into Freemasonry. He seemed quite pleased with what I had discovered since our last meeting.

"You have come up with some very interesting arguments, many of which I have not heard before."

He then went on to invite me to a series of forthcoming Masonic seminars outside of the centre, which he suggested might hold information relevant to my search. Without hesitation I accepted and attended the seminar run by Professor Cecile Revauger, from the Université de Bordeaux III.

The Mystery System

It was only after I had attended the whole series of seminars that I sort of understood what Freemasonry was all about. Even though there was often a sore lack of evidence for some of the more tantalising conclusions put forward by the academics, I could not help but agree with most of their theories. For instance, it was stated that the craft of Freemasonry was born out of a fraternal network of craft lodges, which were originally developed by the medieval stonemasons or artisans. And that these stonemasons constructed their awesome religious temples, the Gothic Minsters and Cathedrals, using a Hermetic mystery-system that can still be found, hidden, not only within their elaborate architecture, but also in Freemasonry teachings. In one of the seminars it was even proposed that the stonemasons' mystery system was composed of three distinct yet interrelated parts.

The first part of the mystery system dealt with the sacred geometry that can be found in all natural forms, such as honeycombs, and in the perfect symmetry of a single snow crystal. This particular part of the system taught that the essence of God's 'sacred geometry', which was rendered into the architecture of Gothic temples,[1] could also be found within the design of plants, animals and in the construct of the human form itself. I remember listening intently as the Mason explained to the audience that this idea was championed throughout time by visionaries such as Pythagoras, Plato, Euclid and Fibonacci.

The second part of the stonemasons' mystery system sat with the events surrounding the building of King Solomon's Temple. Here the early stonemasons believed that Solomon's Temple was quite literally a personification of God's inspiration on earth; its divine architecture being the metaphorical blueprint for the medieval Minsters and Cathedrals. It was also proposed that the stonemasons carved images of the 'magic' story surrounding the building of Solomon's Temple into the walls of their Gothic temples, which we will be looking at in the next degree.

As for the third part of the mystery-system, it dealt with the influence of Paganism on early religious beliefs. According to the high ranking Mason dealing with this issue, examples of this part of the system could also be found within Minsters and Cathedrals, in the form of ethereal icons, such as the Green Man (fig. 51).

Figure 51

The Mason even proposed that the Gothic temple was an archive of esoteric knowledge or secret symbolism in stone. He captivated the audience with a single, profound statement.

"The word 'temple', from the Latin *tempus*, simply means 'time'."

Secrets in the Guild

The most intriguing theory that was delivered through the seminars dealt with the select group of medieval-French stonemasons that constructed the first Gothic Minsters and Cathedrals. According to the doctor delivering the seminar, these stonemasons were descendants of the Gnostics from Egypt and the Holy land, who fled from their Roman persecutors in the 2nd century.

With my digital recorder switched on, the doctor explained his theory.

"The text that provides the background for this theory is called *On the Detection and Overthrow of Gnosis*, which was similarly written in the 2nd century by the Bishop of Lyon."

These initial words made me think of the Swiss magic doctor's theory, which suggested that the *Lost Testament of Solomon* was taken to southern France by the fleeing Gnostics for safe keeping.

"These early Gnostics survived in southern France for many centuries. Their esoteric knowledge was preserved and passed down through the ages, until the time of the medieval, Gnostic stonemasons, who ultimately used it to help construct their sacred-geometric temples. These stonemasons were part of the so-called Gnostic-Albigensian movement, which tried to promote its Gnostic beliefs to the masses, with support from prominent families and nobles, such as Raymond V, Count of Toulouse. This angered the Catholic Church, and so with help from the northern French Barons they literally wiped the Gnostic movement from the face of the earth, in the so-called Albigensian Crusade. Many of the Gnostics who survived the genocide were left to wander Europe; some hiding again

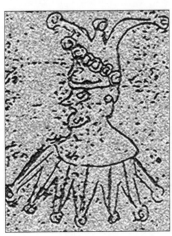

Figure 52

in the trades and guilds, such as stonemasonry and papermaking, while others became the original troubadour gypsy players, who preserved their esoteric knowledge in songs and plays."

To give weight to this idea, the doctor projected an image of a paper watermark onto the white screen, from a medieval-Gnostic manuscript (fig. 52).

"Before their persecution, the earliest paper making centres in Europe were controlled by the Albigensian Gnostics. After their persecution, many of them were re-employed by the open-minded Knights Templar network to keep the important craft alive. This Gnostic watermark depicts the travelling troubadour, jester or Gnostic fool; fool being a derogatory term now, but in the thirteenth century it meant someone who proposes mad ideas, ideas not in line with the Catholic doctrines, Gnostic ideas."

For some reason I thought back to my conversation about the misericords with the old guide at Beverley Minster, playing back his words in my mind, "Like my father told me, only the eternal Fool goes in search of this particular treasure". Did he mean the Gnostic Fool?

"This secret image of the fool in the paper, which also appears in the Gnostic tarot system, wearing his clown-like cap, represents the plight of the many Albigensians who had turned to making a living using song and dance, whilst passing-on their Gnostic ideas."

At the end of the seminar I approached the doctor and asked if I could take a photograph of the watermark.

"Do you see the Gnostic jester's hat, the fool's cap?" asked the doctor.

"So the Gnostic papermaker's fool's cap has a deeper meaning?"

"That's right. This is where writing paper got its name from, foolscap paper."

"That's really fascinating. I bet very few people know about this. Can I ask, at the beginning of your seminar you also suggested that the Gothic temple holds the key for unlocking the Gnostic mysteries, could you expand on this?"

He lifted the lid of his briefcase, took out a thin book and read out its title.

"*Rosslyn: A History of the Guilds, The Masons and the Rosy Cross*. This work was written by the current Knights Templar Archivist for Scotland, Robert Brydon. He similarly suggests that the Gnostic stonemasons transmuted their esoteric symbolism into a greater permanence of metal, wood and stone, to form their Gothic temples."

He reached into his briefcase again, this time pulling out a much thicker book.

"You might want to source a copy of this comprehensive work, Fulcanelli's master piece, *The Mysteries of Cathedrals: An Esoteric Interpretation of the Hermetic Symbols of the Great Work*."

"So the Gothic temple is a product of the Alchemists' Great Work, the quest to acquire and use the Philosophers' Stone?"

He peered at me over his glasses.

"That's right. The temple is the key-in-stone, the hermetic keystone of the Masonic endeavour, the stone edifice that holds the key for unlocking the Gnostic mysteries."

I quickly explained how I had linked the construction of a temple to the quest to regain Paradise. However, I had to admit that I had not yet worked out how the keyword or Philosophers' Stone could be extracted from the human form to build the temple.

"Maybe your missing link resides with the demonic-Genii fellows who appear in Solomon's temple-building story."

He dipped into his briefcase again and took out a wallet of photographs containing various images of the demonic-Genii (fig. 53).

Figure 53

"As you can see, I have collected an array of Genii-forms from the architecture of Minsters and Cathedrals over the years. If you track down the Old Testament pseudepigraphical work, the *Testament of Solomon*, you will find that it not only describes the qualities and physical attributes of these demons, but it also tells you their names."

"Yes, I know the work quite well. A magic-doctor told..."

"What you might not know is that in 1125 the famous Cistercian monk, St. Bernard, unwittingly made a reference to these stone-carved demonic-Genii in his so-called *Apologie*."

He took out a copy of the *Apologie* from his briefcase and began reading.

"What are these ridiculous monsters, horrible beauties and beautiful horrors doing? What of these impure and monstrous centaurs and half-human beings?"

"So St. Bernard did not know what they were?"

"Of course not. But what you have to realise is that the Genii-spirit in Arabic, Hebrew and especially Roman culture was synonymous with the creative inner-human spirit; you know, the magical power of the *Genii* or *Genie*, the root for the modern word 'genius'? It was thought in such times, and by many today, that humans were composed of a balance between good and evil, or angelic and demonic parts. Just like in Solomon's temple building story, the Genii spirit gives us the ability to construct using knowledge from the Divine."

"Good and evil? Do you mean from the Tree of Knowledge, God's secret knowledge?"

"I never thought about it like that. I suppose you are right." The doctor paused for a long moment. "But if this were the case, then why would God cast us to earth? Why would he not want us to have this knowledge?"

I chuckled to myself.

"Maybe there is more to the *Genesis* story than meets the eye."

"Maybe."

"So, basically, what you are saying is that if we could tap into our inner Genii or genius we could, in effect, build a temple using God's secret knowledge, a divine temple?"

"I suppose it is also worth noting that the word 'Gothic' arcs back to the magic-nature of Solomon's Temple, since it is derived from the ancient Greek word *goeteia*, which simply means 'sorcery' or 'magic'."

"So the stonemason's Gothic temples should really be described as magic temples because they were constructed using the genius or Genii that the stonemasons somehow tapped into?"

"Let's say that you have just made a philosophical observation, based on an ancient spiritual concept."

"I know this might sound like a leap, but do you think that the Gnostic stonemasons were attempting to use their God-given genius to bring heaven to earth via the temple?"

"Well, the art of temple building again arcs back to ancient times, and the hermetic idea of as above, so below would have undoubtedly been part of the Gnostic doctrines."

"But do you think that the Gothic temple was specifically designed to act as a nexus or gateway to access the celestial realm?"

"The Tower of Babel, do you know the story from the Bible?"

"Vaguely."

"They were building a temple in the Mesopotamian city, Babel; a temple that would give them access to the heavens, to Paradise. Of course, I remember now, God says let us go down to destroy the temple. He did not want them to get back to Paradise."

"Us go down?"

"Yes, I assume this means the trinity."

I chuckled to myself again and the doctor placed both hands on his head.

"Yes, a temple nexus. I do believe that the early Rosicrucians were caught-up with a similar idea."

He looked at me in a strange way.

"Hold on, I have an early example of a tracing board for the last of the Rosy Cross Temple Degrees."

Vitruvius and the Philosophers' Stone

While waiting for the doctor to produce the image of the tracing board from his briefcase, I started to wonder just what it would look like. However, before I could even begin to formulate a picture in my mind, he had placed it on the desk (fig. 54).[2]

Figure 54

Using his little finger to illustrate the component parts of the tracing board, he began skirting round the eight-sided rose towards the centre of the image.

"Here we have the Ogdoad version of the Rosicrucian rose, at its centre the cross to signify the all-important Rose Cross. As you can see, the entire image is encapsulated by the square or rational form, while the cross provides the triangular or irrational form. Finally, if you look closely, we have the circle, the transcendental form, which completes the essence of the geometric and mathematical triad."

"Yes, the square, triangle and circle, the Philosophers' Stone."

"Now from these three basic forms, the square, triangle and circle, or rational, irrational and transcendental, we have the basis for the geometric attributes found not only in Gothic temples, but also in Greek temples, Muslim mosques and Jewish synagogues."

He looked at his watch.

"I have to leave for my train now, but I have really enjoyed this conversation, I have even learnt a couple of things."

He closed up his briefcase, shook my hand and headed for the exit. Just before he was about to disappear through the doorway he stopped, turned round and shouted out.

"I think Vitruvius will help you to resolve the temple mystery."

I was buzzing with excitement when, that evening, I began researching Vitruvius, and soon discovered that it was the name of a Roman architect who had produced a work called *De Architectura*, which incorporates a chapter on the proportions of temples. After downloading a copy of the work, I found that Vitruvius believed that the ancient art of temple building was based around the divine proportions found within the human form.[3] He wrote that these proportions could be described as ratios, for the building of a 'perfect' temple, by placing the human form inside a square, triangle and circle – the Philosophers' Stone. By the end of the evening, I also discovered that the Vitruvian Temple-Man had been reinterpreted throughout the ages, at times being united with the design of the heavens or cosmos (fig. 55).[4]

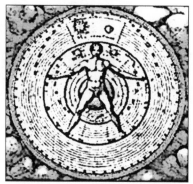

Figure 55

Having dreamt about the Philosophers' Stone that night, the next morning I re-examined the Rosicrucians' version of it (fig. 31); and it was here that I began to see just how the human form could be linked to the construct of a sacred temple using God's Geometric Word. For me, the temple was simply a personification of the divine ratios that were lost or more to the point hidden within our very being:

> Make of the man and woman a Circle, of that a Quadrangle (square), of this a Triangle, of the same a Circle and you will have the Stone of the Philosophers.[5]

Having shared my deepened revelation with George, he at last looked pleased.

Figure 31

"You are on the cusp of unlocking the extent of this ancient mystery. But you still have to reacquire the knowledge that has been with us since our celestial downfall."

George systematically went through each part of the mystery, explaining how the esoteric knowledge associated with the quest to regain Paradise had been preserved and passed down through the ages.

At first he began with the Albion Druids, explaining how they had passed on their 'divine' knowledge to early cultures from the East; knowledge encompassing an esoteric story with a prophetic ending so far reaching that it would haunt the minds of scholars and theologians for millennia to come. He then moved slowly through Egypt and the Holy Land, recounting not only the development of the secret, Gnostic story surrounding master plan of the Immortal Man of Light, but also the nature of the temple building process that would one day be used to access the celestial realm. He then turned to 2nd century France, where he explained how the mystery had been preserved, until it was encoded into the metal, wood and stone of Gothic temples. He spent much time focusing on the White Rabbit, Cherubin, and the prophesised adepts who would one day take part in the final battle and complete the quest to regain Paradise (fig. 56). Finally, he described the 'modern' leg of the quest, making light of the mysterious teachings of the demonic-magicians, Rosicrucians and Freemasons, while paying homage to people like Isaac Newton, William Blake, Godfrey Higgins and even Lewis Carroll; all of which had played a part in preserving the mystery for future generations to rediscover. After all this George flipped over a book on his desk to reveal a strange title, which he read out.

Figure 56

"*Anacalypsis: An Enquiry into the Origins of Language, Nations and Religions*, by Godfrey Higgins."

He opened it to a marked page and began reading a passage that described the existence of a druidical temple building system, which Higgins had unearthed in the mysterious teachings of Freemasonry.

"My Masonic friends will find their craft very often referred to, however they will not find any of their secrets betrayed; but I trust they will find it proved that their art is the remains of a very fine ancient system."

He slammed the book shut.

"You are now part of the legacy, and I suppose you can do something that I should have done years ago; you can give the mystery to the masses."

"Maybe I could write a book George, and you could be the main character."

Figure 57

George dipped into his jacket pocket and pulled out what looked like a postcard, which he skimmed across the top of his desk. As it span towards me I could clearly see the Ogdoad-signature. I saved it from falling off the desk with a slap, just like in the movies (fig.57).

"It's a sun clothed Jesus inside the Ogdoad rose."

"So what's next then George?"

"Well, the key you require to solve this mystery, Milton's golden key, resides within the Minster's architecture, but it is Gothic."

"So you're saying there's a golden key hidden within the Gothic or should I say magic architecture of the Minster?"

"I can tell you little else. You are now in possession of all the facts. So be off with you, and don't come back until you have found the golden key that will give you access not only to the Lost Word of God, but also to the gateway itself."

11th Degree

The Pathway to Paradise

The day after my conversation with George, Fulcanelli's 'master piece', *The Mysteries of Cathedrals: An Esoteric Interpretation of the Hermetic Symbols of the Great Work*, dropped through my door. To be honest, it was hard going at first, but I eventually came across the idea proposed by the doctor, in that the word 'Gothic' came from the ancient Greek word *goeteia*, meaning 'magic.' Captivated by the idea, I turned again to the early European demonic-magic texts, and soon found an old work aptly called *Goetia*[1] or 'Magic'.

Gothic Magic

What intrigued me about *Goetia* was that it not only held a description of the 72 demonic-Genii that Solomon used to build his temple, but also a description of the 72 angels of God that were employed to keep them in check. The idea being that the comparable number of good and evil entities would serve to maintain the celestial balance.

After reading about this celestial balancing act and events surrounding the building of Solomon's Temple, I turned again to the *Testament of Solomon*. Here I found myself focusing on the episode where Solomon was given the ring on behalf of the Gnostic god Sabaoth, to help enslave the demonic-Genii so they would build his temple:

Take, O Solomon, king, son of David wear this seal of God... And this engraving of the seal of the ring sent thee is a Pentalpha [Pentacle].[2]

Having seen something about Solomon's Pentalpha seal when looking at the astronomical relationship between Venus and the rose-pentacle, I turned to my notes and discovered a geo-numeric connection between the seal and the 72 angels and demons. For instance, Solomon's Pentalpha seal was naturally divided by 5 lots of 72 degrees (fig. 58).

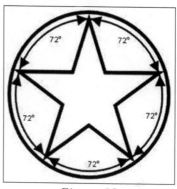

Figure 58

I could not help but think that the seal had been used on Solomon's ring as it encompassed the number found in the demonic-angelic balance. That is, a talisman divided by 72 degrees to represent the 72 angels and demons. While looking into this idea, I also found that the Pentalpha seal was traditionally used at the end of a fairy-angel's magic wand to repel demons, and that it was still used in the art of necromancy to summon demons. Unaware that I had unearthed one of the last and most profound pieces of the esoteric jigsaw, I filed my findings away and started preparing for my next move, which was to visit the source.

It was just after Christmas in 2005 when I casually strolled into the stonemasons' courtyard at York Minster. I approached the only door with a buzzer and pressed it. After introducing myself over the intercom, I was invited into the offices and met with a gentleman who was obviously intrigued by the nature of my enquiry.

"*Gothic* means 'magic' then. I suppose this makes sense," the gentleman began after ten minutes listening to my take on the connection between Freemasonry and stonemasonry. He then asked a question which immediately made the hairs on the back of my neck stand to attention. "I suppose you are already aware of the fable surrounding the angels and demons that is attached to the design of the stained glass supports in the Chapter House?"

"No, I am not. I see I have come to the right place."

He reached over to the shelf behind him and took out a scroll of paper. In a matter of seconds he was spreading out a detailed sketch of the stained glass supports from the Chapter House across his desk.

"I was once told that these supports hold the seventy-two names of the angels of God."

"So the angels' names are carved into the stone supports?"

"Not exactly. I believe their names are somehow encoded into the geometry of the supports to repel demons."

I continued to question him about this issue, but he had little else to offer.

"Could I take a copy of the plans? I assure you, if I can crack the angelic code you will be the first to know."

He accepted.

That afternoon I set about examining the geometry of the supports in the Chapter House, but soon realised that if they did contain an angelic code, I would struggle to crack it. As you can see with one of the eight identical supports from the Chapter House, the geometric forms or discs are based around the numbers 5 and 9 (fig. 59).

Figure 59

After an hour or so thinking about who I could ask for help, I emailed an image of the supports and an appropriate explanation to the centre dedicated to research into Freemasonry. To my surprise, I soon after received an extensive email response from a high ranking Mason based in Lincoln, who had done some work on the images. He began by explaining that the geometric shapes in the Chapter House were specifically put there to hide a sacred form. For example, in his first image he illustrated the existence of two Pentalpha (fig. 60).

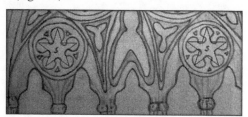

Figure 60

I must admit, I was a little surprised to read that the Mason likened this arrangement to the angelic-demonic celestial balance of 72 degrees, which he referred to as "the eternal, sacred equilibrium between dark and light forces". He also explained that the idea of angels and demons was not just something that appeared in magic texts and religious buildings, but also in films and cartoons, where an angel and demon sit on the shoulders of an earthly being to portray a moral dilemma. Again, I could not help but think about the idea of us eating from the Tree of Knowledge; a tree containing God's secret knowledge, good and evil, the balance of the celestial forces.

The Mason also proposed that the geometry in the stained glass supports held, "a rare example of the Ennead that is usually reserved for the highest of all Masons, the 33 Degree Mason". Here he explained that, "This rare example of the nine-sided form is undoubtedly representative of the perfect trinity of the Nine Gods or the Ennead, which can be found in Egyptian, Gnostic, Hermetic-Rosicrucian and Freemasonry teachings." To help illustrate the Ennead form, he provided an image of the 33 degree Masonic medal, alongside the appropriate geometry in the Chapter House supports (fig. 61).

Figure 61

Intrigued by the idea of the Ennead, I decided to phone the Mason, in hope that he would explain why it appeared in the Chapter House alongside the two Pentalpha.

"Yes, it's quite fascinating what you have discovered," he began. "The geometry obviously reflects the nine points of light or the angelic essence that makes-up the Ennead."

"Nine points of light? Angelic essence?"

"Yes, the nine points of light are there to denote the special Shem Ha-Mephorash calculation that was known to the enlightened ones, which appears not only in the *Book of Exodus*, but also in occult tarot, Kabbalistic teachings, and even in the ceiling of the Sistine Chapel in the Vatican."[3]

"Shem Ha-Mephorash calculation?"

"The calculation that reveals the angelic essence of God, His Lost Word."

"So you are saying that the geometry in the supports contains the Lost Word of God?"

Realising that this was somewhat of a revelation to me, his tone changed.

"Traditionally, the Word of God was composed using the names of the 72 angels. Here each angel had a three-letter name, and so God's Word was composed of 216 letters, or if you like 72 three-letter names."

"216, 6x6x6, that's the Number of the Beast isn't it? 216, it's both good and evil, the balance."

"I don't know about that, but you have definitely discovered a rare, if not unique example of the Lost Word in religious architecture. I believe it could be quite significant for many organisations, but not so popular with the Church."

"So how can I read the Lost Word of God from the Chapter House supports?"

"Well, with what you now know it should be easy to work out. All you have to do is calculate the number of letters; that's the circular nodes or points of light in each Ennead."

"I still don't get it."

"Look, I'll mail you something that will help, and don't underestimate yourself."

In order to explain how I found the Lost Word of God on that fateful evening in 2005, I first need to point out again how the Ennead appears in the Chapter House (fig. 62). As you can see, each of the eight compartments holds three-Ennead, which sit at the pinnacle of the stained glass windows.

Figure 62

In the first instance, considering that each point of light or node represented an angelic letter, I worked out how many letters were in each compartment. I simply multiplied 3 by 9 to get 27 letters. In order to work out the total number of letters from the 8 compartments, I then multiplied 27 by 8. As I finished typing the numbers into my calculator I paused, and with a sudden rush of excitement pressed the equals-button... After staring at the truly 'magic' number (216) for several moments, I printed out eight copies of the compartment and laid them out side-by-side (fig. 63)

Figure 63

As I was staring at the geometric version of the Shem Ha-Mephorash or Lost Word of God, it suddenly dawned on me that I could prove its existence in the Chapter House. All I had to do was divide 216 by the number of letters in an angel's name (3), to give me the number of angels (72).

I again turned to the calculator, which still held the value 216, and pressed the division sign, followed by the number 3. I again paused over the equals-button, and this time with a sense of inevitability pressed it. Having gloated for a while about the appearance of 72 on the screen, I was suddenly distracted

•	7	6	5	4	3	2	1	
כהת	אכא	ללה	מהש	עלם	סיט	ילי	והו	1
הקם	הרי	מבה	יזל	ההע	לאו	אלד	הוי	2
ההו	מלה	יי	נלכ	פהל	לוו	כלי	לאו	3
רשר	לכב	אום	ריי	שאה	ירח	האא	נתה	4
יי	רהע	חעם	אני	מגד	כוק	להת	יזו	5
מיה	עשל	ערי	סאל	ילה	ול	סיכ	ההה	6
פוי	מבה	ניח	ננא	עמם	החש	דני	והו	7
מחי	ענו	יהה	ומב	מצר	הרח	ייל	נמם	8
מום	היי	יבמ	ראה	תבו	איע	מנק	רמב	9

Figure 64

by my computer mail-received notification, which is customised to a high-pitched voice saying "Dickey Boy you have mail!" On opening the email, which had been sent by the Mason, I found that he had attached a grid containing the 216 letters or three-letter names of the 72 angels, the Lost Word of God (fig. 64).

What initially struck me about the grid was its 8 by 9 arrangement. I could not help but think about the overall geometry in the Chapter House, which was formed to represent the Ogdoad (8), the home of the gods, while at the same time it incorporated the Ennead (9), the gods themselves. So with this in mind I quickly multiplied the two numbers together (8x9) and was once again faced with the number 72.

The Golden Key for Unlocking the Lost Word of God

The next morning, unable to contain myself, I phoned the Mason to tell him my news. He sounded very enthusiastic.

"I must admit I am starting to see just how important this might be, I need to mail you a copy of all the Masonic Ennead Degrees, the first of which is called the *Elu of Nine*."[4]

"The Ennead Degrees?"

"In the last of the Ennead Degrees, that of the *Grand Elect, Perfect and Sublime Elu*, the candidate is given the Lost Word of God. I will also mail you a copy of the temple tracing board that holds the Shem Ha-Mephorash calculation."

Having received the email later that morning, I immediately opened the image of the temple tracing board (fig. 65). Initially my eyes were drawn to the familiar Ennead nine-form, which sat at the centre of the scene. I then turned to the eight Corinthian columns, which the Mason described in his email as "a representation or allusion to the Ogdoad Chapter". I had no need to multiply the Ogdoad and Ennead together, since I already knew the answer.

Figure 65

Later in the day, I discovered that one of the Ennead Degrees, the *Royal Arch of Enoch*, *Master of the Ninth Arch*, dealt with King Solomon's discovery of the Lost Word. It was whilst reading through this degree that I found a fascinating connection between George's latest riddle, regarding Milton's golden key and the Chapter House. According to the degree, once King Solomon had taken possession of the Lost Word, he made a golden key and inscribed it with the words *In arc leonis verbum inveni*, which means, 'In the lion's mouth I found the Word'. He then locked the Word in the Arc of the Covenant with the key and gave it to a magical lion to swallow.

When I first read about this event, a familiar picture of a prominent carving from the Chapter House came to the forefront of my mind. I am sure you can imagine my elation when I made my way down to the Chapter House to see the carving, and saw one of the anonymous adepts looking for the key in the lion's mouth (fig. 66).

Figure 66

Revealing the Ennead

Excited by what I'd discovered, I made my way to the shop, to share my revelation. Inevitably, George had much to add.

"Yes, many seekers will discover the location of the key, but it is only the prophesised adepts who are destined to use it." He began waving his finger round like an insane conductor and suddenly burst into song. "Three is the magic number."

"Look, I've had enough of the riddles George; can you be straight with me for just once?"

He smiled, stood up, and moved towards the glass cabinet at the back of the shop. He reached inside and took out what looked like an old parchment. I was hopeful that he would at last show me the extent of the prophesy.

"This Gnostic-magic work was unearthed in Egypt, Chenoboskion, Nag Hammadi, it is known as *Hermes Trismegistus' Discourse on the Eighth and Ninth*."

"What, Hermes Trismegistus, the equivalent of Ningizzida, Lord of the Tree of Life?"

"It holds a description of how the prophesised Gnostic-adepts will use their degrees of knowledge to not only acquire immortality, but also gain access to the great gods in the celestial realm. In order to do this they first have to understand the nature of the realm of the gods, the Ogdoad eight, because this will ultimately reveal the gods themselves, the Ennead nine."

He cleared his throat and began to read from the work.

"It is thus by degrees that the adepts will enter into the way of immortality and will attain to a conception of the Ogdoad, which in turn reveals the Ennead."

"So the geometry associated with the Ogdoad and Ennead must have been purposely executed by the stonemasons in the Chapter House. They must have known."

"Yes, the Chapter House was built so that the adepts can physically or perhaps metaphorically achieve their ultimate goal; gain immortality and stand before the Authorities to take back the ultimate prize, Paradise."

X Marks the Spot

After spending a few days considering the gravity of what I had discovered, I again had a good look through everything that I had collected over the years. In doing this, I came to the Rosicrucian or Rosy Cross emblem that holds the temple-signature (fig. 54). Initially, I focused on the Messiah at the centre of the Ogdoad-rose, who offers immortality and the chance to return to the celestial realm. But what stood out, with my new eyes, was that the centre of the rose-cross was obscured or perhaps hidden

Figure 54

by the Messiah; and with what seemed like a surge of divine inspiration, I realised that 'X' traditionally denoted the location of the treasure.

I started to consider that, if the rose-cross did mark the spot of the treasure, then to 'cross' the Vitruvian-Temple Man might reveal some sort of clue. So I turned to the most famous adaptation of the Vitruvian-Temple Man, which many suggest was produced by a member of the Rosicrucian Order, Leonardo da Vinci.[5] I then placed it alongside the temple signature and crossed the square to reveal something quite unexpected.

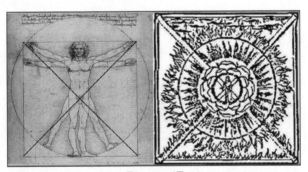

Figure 67

After a little giggle to myself, I began to wonder just why Leonardo da Vinci had portrayed the Vitruvian-Temple Man inside the square and circle, but had chosen not to cross it. I knew that the square represented earth and the circle heaven. So how did the cross fit in? As the answer came to me, I spoke it out loud.

"To cross the square and circle is to cross from earth to heaven, to join the two together, to create the nexus, it's the missing link. By crossing the square and circle the gateway is revealed."

With the cross in place, the Vitruvian-Temple Man had come to life. He was quite literally the personification of a temple that had been produced to reproduce; a human temple that held an intrinsic, secret knowledge that would one day be used to create and ultimately pass through the gateway to Paradise.

12th Degree

The Temple Enigmas

It was in the summer of 2006 when George phoned to explain that he was shutting up shop due to poor health, so I decided that it was time to put my findings into words. It was time to go it alone. Not being a writer as such I found it very difficult to get going, but after a couple of years things started to come together. There was no need to embellish the facts, all I had to do was tell the truth, and write down what I had witnessed. And by the summer of 2008 I had basically finished, but for one important thing, a truly profound ending. So in a melancholy state I put down my keyboard and started to consider if there was anything else to be done. Had I found all there was to be found? Or was there just one more clue to be discovered that would lead to a final resolution?

The House of Houses

After a year or so searching, nothing was forthcoming. So in a last ditch attempt, in December, 2009, I headed for the Minster. Once I had trawled through the Gothic structure for an hour or so, I spent a good while sitting in its octagonal temple without any sort of resolution. Defeated, I stood up and began to make my way out.

As I left, I carried out my usual routine. But, after wedging a golden coin into the lion's mouth and bowing my head to the guardians of the gateway, I noticed something that I had never really considered before; a Latin inscription between two marble columns, just next to the door that lead to the secret,

Figure 68

Rosicrucian room. I pulled out my trusty camera and took a couple of shots (fig. 68).

When I got back home, I set-about trying to translate the inscription, but ended-up emailing a copy to my dad. A few hours later, whilst in the kitchen, I heard my mail-received notification sound out, "Dickey Boy you have mail!" I opened the e-mail and read the translation (fig. 69).

Figure 69

With my mind racing, an image of Venus as the astronomical rose suddenly flashed before my eyes, and then the rose-cross itself, the cross that marked the spot of the ultimate temple treasure. It was in this sublime moment that I knew I had spent the last two decades of my life wisely. I had discovered the house of houses, the temple of all temples. I was convinced that I had found the final clue to a five-thousand year old mystery; a mystery that centred on the ultimate quest of the human race, the quest to regain Paradise.

The next morning I was the first person into the Minster and made my way across to the Chapter House. Just as I was about to enter the corridor leading to the octagonal temple, I came face to face with the Archbishop of York. Even though I intuitively knew that he would not appreciate what I was about to say to him, I smiled anyway.

"I believe I have found the gateway to Paradise, it is here in the Chapter House."

"Yes," he laughed. "Of course if you have discovered the gateway to Paradise, then the implications are perhaps as far reaching as discovering God Himself, it could literally change everything, the greatest story never told I think."

He laughed again, raised his arms and pointed to the two globe-shaped lights that were illuminating the entrance to the corridor. Somehow mesmerised by the lights, all I could do was listen to the dragging of the Archbishop's garb on the stone floor as he made his way towards the heart of the Minster. As my eyes became accustomed to light, I saw that each globe was resting on a hybrid figure, between them a massive pentacle hidden within the geometry of the carved stone. It was the griffins, guarding the entrance to the corridor that led to the gateway.

I made my way into the Chapter House and took up position at its centre, within the small, tiled octagon, which I immediately realised held an image of the fruit from the Tree of Life. I turned around full-circle and noticed that the floor tiles were branching out to form X-shaped crosses, stretching out to meet the icon-rich, stone walls. I was standing at the intersection, where X marked the spot. Moved by what seemed like a divine force I turned to the east, closed my eyes and tilted my head towards the heavens, to the pinnacle of the octagonal structure, where the Ogdoad fuses with the Ennead. I stood there, waiting. I waited some more... nothing.

It suddenly came to me. I was standing at the centre of a temple portal, a time portal, a tempus, an archive of human knowledge cut out of stone. And they were all looking at me, the ancients; the multitude of weird and wonderful faces adorning the octagonal edifice. They were all watching me as their faces began to shine with the light from the rising sun. I could see the entire mystery before my eyes. I could taste it, feel it, as if it was part of my very being. But, alas, there was still something missing.

The Agents

While at work the next day I got into a conversation with a man called Ned Hoste, who had dropped in to do some creative design work with our 6th form technology students. On hearing that he ran a design consultancy, 2H Design, with much experience in design for book publishing, I started to quiz him. In short, this conversation led me to contact a man called Gary Smailes; a historian, extensively published author, once researcher for Horrible Histories writer Terry Deary and member of BubbleCow, a company set up to help new writers get published. In due course I sent my work to him for an appraisal, and he seemed quite excited about it, offering some excellent advice on how I might improve its flow and pace, and most importantly, how to create a book proposal to send to literary agents, the gatekeepers of the literary world.

A few weeks later, after a little restructuring, I tentatively mailed my book proposal – a covering letter, synopsis and the first three chapters – through cyberspace to an agent from Northern Ireland called Paul Feldstein. I chose him for a very specific reason. The colophon or logo on his website held a mosaic containing a griffin guardian. To my delight Paul emailed me back the following day to explain that he was intrigued by my proposal and that he would like to take a look at the entire work, so I promptly emailed it to him.

Feeling helpless, my 'Gnostic revelation' in the hands of a stranger, I decided to look into what made Paul tick, so if he did like my work and phoned to 'check me out', I could somehow use what I had discovered to impress him. At least that's how I saw it at the time.

After reading a feature about him on an Irish cultural website,[1] I found that he had a bit of a thing for W.B. Yeats. So I set about looking into the antics of this legendary, literary character, and to my surprise discovered that Yeats had not only been mixed up with Hermetic-Rosicrucianism, but was also admitted to the Order of the Golden Dawn, and had been influenced greatly by the esoteric works of William Blake, calling him one of the "great artificers of God who uttered great truths to a little clan".[2] It all seemed perfect, almost as if it was part of the mystery itself.

While browsing the online exhibition of the Life and Works of Yeats at the National Library of Ireland,[3] I found a display cabinet in the Celtic Mystic section that held a selection of Golden Dawn tarot cards, talismans and ritual notebooks. As I clicked through the pages of one of the more interesting notebooks,[4] I found several references to and images of the caduceus, which had been overlaid onto a Cabalistic version of the Tree of life. Spurred on by these examples of the ancient, esoteric connection between the caduceus and the Tree of Life, I eventually came to a description of the layout for the temple, on page 65 of the notebook, as part of the 9th degree, which depicts the Tree of Life at the centre of the temple. Having stood on a depiction of the fruit from the Tree of Life at the centre of the temple of all temples, it made me consider that I had discovered yet another important part of the mystery. Could it be that obvious, could the Tree of Life, the caduceus, reside at the centre of the temple, where X marks the spot?

Unfortunately, Paul decided that my work was not for him. In a way I was devastated, but soon after made another inspired approach to an agent called Robin Wade, from Wade & Doherty Literary Agency, based in London. Within a couple of days I had again secured a full read, and then an email back from Robin saying he believed my work was "eminently publishable". He also suggested that I might have missed something important:

Several years ago someone approached me with a similar idea in a very different context. It seemed a little weird at the time, so I decided not to run with it. For instance, you showed us the 72 angelic names in Hebrew, but don't try to decode them. My instinct is that the geometric discs in the Chapter House can be used to form some kind of Enigma machine. I bet you could find a retired GCHQ code-breaker who would relish this challenge or at least quickly disprove that the shapes could be turned into a machine of sorts. I suggest you look into this and then get back to me.

I emailed Robin back to say that I would look into his interesting idea about the machine over the next week or so. I also mentioned his idea to a colleague at school, a guy called Steve Teasdale, who has many links with WW2 veterans; and in his role as aviation artist produced the official painting for the 60th anniversary of the Great Escape. Steve explained that he would be at the Duxford Flying Legends Air Show that weekend, and that if I put something together to explain the machine idea, he would ask around for anyone who knew of a code breaker or some such like.

So I put everything onto a pen drive with my contact details and an explanatory note and passed it to him. To my delight, on the following Monday, Steve explained that he had given the pen drive to one of his contacts that knew a once member of the Eagle Squadron in World War Two, whose wife worked at Bletchley Park at the time of the Enigma machine. Unable to work out how to put any sort of Enigma-type machine together using the geometric discs, I spent the rest of the week hoping that someone would make contact.

I was just about to leave for work on the Friday morning of that week when the letterbox clattered. As I opened the door to exit, I picked up the red and white card that had been posted by Royal Mail, with a tick next to the box indicating that they had a parcel that was too big to post. All through the day I was a little distracted, thinking about what the parcel might be. As soon as the final bell rang and I had completed bus duty, I made my way over to the delivery office, handed over the card and after a minute or so was handed a heavy, flat, rectangular object over a meter in length, wrapped in corrugated cardboard.

As soon as I got outside I carefully ripped away at one corner to reveal what looked like a cog with Hebrew letters inscribed onto each tooth. Brimming with a strange feeling of anxiety and excitement, I quickly placed the package on the back seat of the car and headed for home. Once inside I frantically ripped away at the cardboard to reveal what I can only describe as a Hebrew Enigma machine (fig. 70). It was absolutely amazing. But who had sent it?

Figure 70

The Enigma Wheel of Fortune

Wedged underneath one of the cogs was a disc, which I assumed contained information about the machine. So I turned on my computer, put in the disk and clicked on the only file, entitled, "eyesonly":

The system you have discovered in the eight window compartments is based on a three tier Pascaline system. This system holds the usual series of eight horizontal cogs but with the two extra tiers, adding to its complexity. The cogs have to be placed vertically so they function as a machine. As they stand they would not turn but the intention is quite obvious and I will explain why as we move on using a Cabbalistic methodology that correlates to the Lost Word of God calculation in *Exodus*.

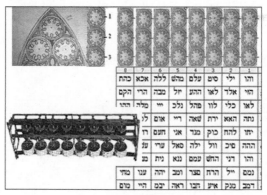

Figure 71

The 72 angelic names are secreted within the well-known *Exodus* story that tells of the parting of the Red Sea as described in the 3 sections, *Exodus* 14: 19, 20 and 21. The ancient Cabbalists decoded the 72 names from *Exodus* writing the first of the three sections right to left, the second left to right and the third right to left. The relevance of this will become apparent in a moment in terms of the natural movement of each train of cogs. The table below shows how the angelic grid works as a three tier Pascaline system, mimicking the exact setup in the 8 window compartments in the Chapter House. Here, C1, C2, C3, C4, C5, C6, C7 and C8 represent the 8 compartments, and 1.1, 1.2 and 1.3, for example, represent the three geometric discs in the first compartment, each containing nine nodes, or in the case of the machine the first three cogs, each with nine teeth.

C8	C7	C6	C5	C4	C3	C2	C1
8.1	7.1	6.1	5.1	4.1	3.1	2.1	1.1
8 כָּהַת	7 אָכָא	6 לֶלֶה	5 מַהֲשׁ	4 עֶלֶם	3 סִי טֵ	2 לִי	1 וְהוּ
16 הַק מ	15 הֲרִי	14 מְבַה	13 יֵזַל	12 הַהַע	11 לָאַו	10 אָלַד	9 הַזִי
24 חֲהַן	23 מְלַה	22 י י ו	21 נְלַכָ	20 פֶהַל	19 לָוַו	18 כָּלִי	17 לָאַו
8.2	7.2	6.2	5.2	4.2	3.2	2.2	1.2
32 וְשַׁר	31 לְכָב	30 אֲנֶמ	29 רִי י	28 שָׁאה	27 יְרֵת	26 הַאָא	25 נְתָה
40 י י	39 רְהַע	38 חֲעֶמ	37 אֲנִי	36 מְגֵד	35 כָּוַק	34 לְהַח	33 י חֲו
48 מִי ה	47 עֲשַׁל	46 עֲרִי	45 סָאַל	44 יְלָה	43 וְוַל	42 מִי כָ	41 הַהַה
8.3	7.3	6.3	5.3 – 1.9	4.3	3.3	2.3	1.3
56 פַן	55 מְבַה	54 נִי תַ	53 נְנָא	52 עֲמֶמ	51 הַחַשׁ	50 דְנִי	49 וְהַו
64 מְחִי	63 עֲנָו	62 י הַה	61 וְמַב	60 מְצֵר	59 הַרַח	58 י י ל	57 נְמַמ
72 מְנַמ	71 הַי י	70 י בַמ	69 רָאָה	68 חֲבַן	67 אַיע	66 מְנַק	65 דְמַב

Figure 72

So, each cog or geometric shape contains three angelic names or nine letters. As the grid dictates, moving from right to left, the first, second and third row of angelic names are assigned to the top row of eight cogs, making 72 letters; the fourth, fifth and sixth row of angelic names to the middle row of cogs, making 72 letters, and the seventh, eighth and ninth row of angelic names to the bottom row of cogs, making 72 letters, completing the sequence of 72 names or 216 letters (3x72).

You do need a cipher to reveal the divine message which I will explain in a moment, but to read from the cogs you need a start point which in this case begins with the first angelic letter assigned to each cog, as defined by the grid. If you look at the physical system that I adapted from a similar system I manufactured several years ago, you will see that I have placed a black dot on each cog and a dot on the board next to each cog to denote the start point alignment. All you need to do now is turn the cog based on the cipher to reveal the message.

Traditionally the cipher for this type of three tier system has 2 digits. The first digit relates to the number of teeth-turns clockwise, allowing you to read in the Hebrew fashion, in this case right to left. As you turn the first cog the second cog will naturally turn anticlockwise, and the third clockwise. Obviously this is describing the natural movement of the train of cogs – the same way the Cabbalists decoded the 72 names from the sections in *Exodus*. So, on the first train of cogs in C1, a possible cipher could be 5, 1. Here, 5 would indicate the number of turns or tooth increments, and 1 would indicate the cog from which to read the letter, the first or top cog in this case. The letter in question would be read from the black dot on the board adjacent to the cog.

After contacting an old code-breaking friend at the Vatican, who has an interest in such ancient systems, he explained that the following cipher would reveal the message that you are undoubtedly seeking from *Exodus* that relates to the Lost Word of God, which has been recognised as the greatest exegetical challenge in the Bible: I AM THAT I AM. But who is He? Spin the Enigma Wheel of Fortune and you may just find out.

C8	C7	C6	C5	C4	C3	C2	C1
4,1	7,1	6,1	5,1	4,1	3,1	2,1	1,1
8,2	7,2	6,2	5,2	4,2	3,2	2,2	1,2
8,3	7,3	6,3	5,3	4,3	3,3	2,3	1,3
1,2	6,2	8,2	2,3	3,1	5,1	5,2	5,1
X?	X?	X?	X?	X?	X?	X?	X?

Figure 73

I will not spoil or should I say spell it out for you, I'll let you work it out for yourself. As a side point, this general concept can also be found where X marks the spot, Tarot card X, the Wheel of Fortune, and in most Ogdoad Hindu and Buddhist mandalas. But I believe your example is probably the most sophisticated and quite special. At least that's how my friend sees it. It is also worth pointing out that the Hebrew alphabet contains 27 letters or three rows of 9 letters, which again equates to the number of nodes in each compartment, or teeth on a train of cogs. Spooky, don't you think. No thanks required. I've enjoyed helping. The Hebrew alphabet table below will be of use.

ט Tet 9	ח Het 8	ז Zayen 7	ו Vav 6	ה He 5	ד Dalet 4	ג Gimel 3	ב Bet 2	א Alef 1	9
צ Tsadi 18	פ Pe 17	ע Ayin 16	ס Samekh 15	נ Nun 14	מ Mem 13	ל Lamed 12	כ Kaf 11	י Yod 10	9
ץ Tsadi 27	ף Pe 26	ן Nun 25	ם Mem 24	ך Kaf 23	ת Tav 22	ש Shin 21	ר Resh 20	ק Qof 19	9

Figure 74

Immediately I set about aligning the machine, twisting each train of cogs so that all the dots matched up. I then began with the first compartment (C1). As I moved the top cog one tooth right, clockwise, the second cog moved to the left and the third to the right. My eyes were darting around, trying to make sense of the strange, rotating characters that had somehow come to life.

Two, three, four, five and stop.

"5, 1," I said under my breath.

I looked to the symbol on the top cog, next to the black dot, the Hebrew letter Yod (י). I had the first letter. Then the next train of cogs, 5, 2, the letter He (ה); then the next, carefully cutting and pasting the Hebrew letters from the table provided by the mysterious source. When I reached the fourth train of cogs I paused for a moment, realising that there was a gap on the board. Had I decoded a four letter Hebrew word? Yod, He, Vav, He, יהוה.

Having used the Google Translate site before to translate a Spanish word, I quickly loaded it up and pasted in the letters. After I clicked "paste" there was a short pause and then the translation appeared on screen. "Wah." Was it a joke? But then I noticed that because of the nature of Hebrew, the translator had swapped the words round, so they read left to right. After a sigh of relief I quickly set about swapping the letters round so they read right to left, and as I pasted in the final letter there was a pause and then the word appeared on screen, "Jehovah".

My first thought was Jehovah's witnesses, so I began a search to see just what Jehovah meant, and quickly discovered that it was the Anglicised version of the Hebrew name for God, Yod, He, Vav, He, or YHVH, with the addition of the appropriate vowels, e, o, and a, to make Yehovah, or as most people spell it, Jehovah.

Impelled to discover the meaning of what I assumed would be another word, I turned the next four cogs and pasted across the four Hebrew letters into Google Translate, Alef, Vav, Resh He, אורה. After rearranging the letters there was a familiar pause and then the English translation appeared on screen, "Light". Clicking on the "listen" button, the word "light" sounded out in an American accent. I pressed it again, and again, "light, light." God and light, I thought. God is light, the Immortal Man of Light?

I turned again to the explanation of the machine, eventually stopping and carefully reading the words, "the following cipher would reveal the message that you are undoubtedly seeking from *Exodus* that relates to the Lost Word of God, which has been recognised as the greatest exegetical challenge in the Bible: I AM THAT I AM. But who is He? Spin the Enigma Wheel of Fortune and you may just find out." Was the mysterious source suggesting that God was light? Immediately the words from a hymn came to mind that my dad had sung on the sunny days when he took me out, as a child, over the mysterious fields of Barnsdale. I sang the hymn out loud.

"Immortal invisible, God only wise, in light inaccessible hid from our eyes. Most blessed, most glorious, the Ancient of Days, almighty, victorious, thy great Name we praise. Great Father of glory, pure Father of light, Thine angels adore Thee, all veiling their sight."

Thy great Name, light, hidden, veiled, I thought, and the term "Ancient of Days" from the hymn somehow seemed familiar, so I typed it into a search engine, clicking on the Wikipedia site dedicated to the phrase. Immediately I was faced with a very familiar painting called the *Ancient of Days* (fig 25); it was William Blake's Grand Architect checking the 'squarness' of his creation, standing in an orb of light that was radiating out, defining his creative expression. For the first time it was all starting to make sense, but, at the same time, what did it all mean?

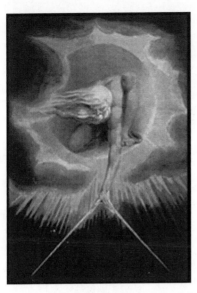

Figure 25

I again turned to the words on the disc. "As a side point, this general concept can also be found where X marks the spot, Tarot card X, the Wheel of Fortune." Absolutely engrossed by what I might discover next, I turned to my computer and typed in "Tarot card X Wheel of Fortune". Again I clicked on the Wikipedia site dedicated to this particular topic and was faced with a picture of a Rosicrucian tarot card (fig. 75), which had been created by A.E. Waite, a member of the Hermetic Order of the Golden Dawn, Societas Rosicruciana in Anglia, and founder of the Fellowship of the Rosy Cross.[5]

As I carefully surveyed the card, it was as if I had somehow become attuned to the esoteric mysteries. Each aspect of the card appeared to me, not as an independent symbol, but as part of an interrelated Gnostic story. At its top, it was denoted as the treasure card, card 'X', and I could clearly see how the Cherubin griffin had been formed, as part of the 'four corners', as described in the Gnostic work, *On the Origins of the World*:

The Cherubin has eight different shapes for each of the four corners, a mix of lion, calf, human and eagle forms. [6]

Just like the Chapter House and other important, ancient edifices, the central wheel was alluding to the eight, to the Ogdoad, at its heart the Name of God from the Hebrew Enigma machine, Yod, He, Vav, He, יהוה; the name that was written into the architecture of the temple itself. But the name was broken up here, separated by the word "ROTA", "הRוOהT'A". So was there something to be gleaned from the word ROTA?

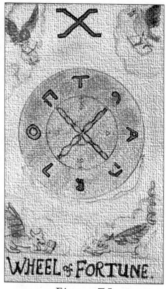

Figure 75

Without hesitation I began a search and soon discovered that the Latin word *rota* meant 'wheel', which is of course used to form words such as rotary and rotate, the basic principle required to reveal the hidden message in the Hebrew Enigma machine. So did the card hold a hidden Gnostic message, solely for those who had understanding? But what could it be?

As I thought about the conundrum, it suddenly dawned on me just how obvious it was. The Wheel of Fortune had to perform its intended function, it had to rotate. So I closed my eyes and began to spin the wheel in my mind, at first focusing on God's name. I could sort of see that, as the wheel spun, God's name was, philosophically, endless, simply going round and round; possibly indicating that within what we might consider to be the wheel of life, God was an integral, elementary part of its construct. Feeling a little dissatisfied with this conclusion, I turned

163

to the word ROTA, writing it out in a line several times "ROTAROTAROTR". I then began moving my eyes across the letters in an attempt to simulate the spinning effect. After a few times back and forth I realised just what the message was, 'ROTAROTAR','TAROT', which I soon discovered was a Hermetic, magical-religious system containing the means by which to access God's secret knowledge, brought to earth by the angelic entities Harut and Marut.[7] But from my perspective this card, which basically defined the essence of tarot, was portraying, in an esoteric sense, the fundamental aspects of the mystery. To me, it was as if I had now discovered another level, a deeper level; unearthing facets of the mystery that I hoped would lead to a final resolution, a resolution to the ultimate quest of the human race.

Not wanting to delay any longer, I emailed Robin Wade to explain what I had discovered. It was all his idea, and I was praying that it would somehow tempt him to offer me representation. After a few hours he mailed me back:

Hi Richard, perhaps you could give me a call in the office on Monday, I will be there from 9 until about 3pm and we can discuss everything? Anyway, have a good weekend and let's chat next week.

School was now out for summer, and it was the first of many Monday mornings of freedom. I picked up the phone then put it down. What was I going to say? My dream of becoming a published author would surely rest on the words that were about to pass over my lips. I took a deep breath and started dialing. It began to ring. Someone picked up.

"Robin Wade."

I paused, maybe for a moment too long.

"Yes, Richard Hewitt. You asked me to call."

"That's right, I did."

"This all seems a little surreal to me Robin."

"And to me too, but probably for a different reason. I must admit, when I read your work I could not stop. I was so intrigued I just had to read it to the end."

As the conversation progressed, I somehow felt that Robin was holding something back. I did not know what, but it eventually came to light after ten minutes.

"So, this machine and everything. Who do you think made it?"

"I'm not sure, but I suppose it would make sense for me to try and contact them."

"But the entire work, all the revelations that you have discovered, do you feel they were fed to you?"

"Fed to me?"

"Yes, you know, someone led you to discover everything, as part of some sort of hidden agenda. In fact, why did you choose to send your work to me? Did someone advise you to?

"Well, I just read your profile on the website and something captured my imagination, the thing about how you came to be published. What do you mean hidden agenda?"

"Do you think that all this was given to you for a reason?"

"George you mean?"

"Maybe."

"What I can say, hand on heart, is that my work is simply an account of my journey to uncover the component parts of the quest to regain Paradise."

Robin suddenly dropped the inquisition and began to explain how he thought the work might be made more appropriate for publishing. But I still felt that something was bothering him, as if his heart was not in it. He kept pausing, and then throwing strange questions at me. After a significant pause I decided to try my luck.

"So what do you really think then? Is it worth pursuing?"

"Of course, yes, absolutely. It's been very good to chat. I'll mail you a copy of our standard agreement for your review."

As I put the phone down it felt like an anticlimax, but at the same time I had done it, I had secured myself an agent. For some reason I felt like Larry David in *Curb Your Enthusiasm*.

Secret Agent

The next day I accessed my new email account and sure enough Robin had emailed me his standard agreement. I had specifically opened this account to deal with issues regarding my book, and so was surprised to see another email in my inbox with the subject heading, "Have You Cracked the Code?" I immediately opened it:

On July 27, BBC 2, 9PM, *The Code* begins. It will touch on many of the things you have discovered, but will not provide a resolution. When you watch the introduction to the program, look out for the labyrinth at Chartres Cathedral, depicting the pathway to the Tree of Life at its centre. Also notice, when it passes by the labyrinth, the shape of Uriel's Machine is highlighted – the two golden bands that illustrate the movement of the sun throughout the solar year. Even though it is not at first obvious, this BBC production marks the beginning of a new zeitgeist that is currently being manufactured to bring to the forefront the concept of intelligent design, the Philosophers' Stone – the idea that hidden within nature are the fingerprints of a Grand Architect.

In *The Code*, Professor Marcus du Sautoy will tell of a powerful code able to "unlock the laws that govern the universe". I have also attached the Tetragrammaton, the Lost Word, which appears on the face of Enoch's triangular Stone with its sacred value decoded, the angelic essence, 72. I would also suggest that you revisit the Gnostic story *On the Origins of the World*. If you read it carefully, you will see that all the entities in the story are in fact made of light. When the Authorities create Adam, they simply take the light and design a container to carry it, a physical body, or as they put it, an "enclosure of light".

There is one aspect of biophoton theory which suggests that these ancient Gnostics were indeed correct. Biophoton light is stored in the cells of every organism, in the DNA, and according to the theory light is constantly released and absorbed by the DNA, connecting everything within the body, creating a communication network to allow all life processes to function. We are in fact made of light. Most pertinently, in *Exodus*, when Moses saw God in the so-called burning bush, it was not burning. This idea is based on a well-known mistranslation. What he actually saw in the bush was pure light, a portal of light, possibly God Himself. Light is the key.

X.

I clicked on the attached image (fig.76), and as it appeared on screen my earlier research came flooding back. The Name of God corresponded to the Lost Word of God, 72, the angelic essence; the Word that could be used to unlock God's secret knowledge in us.

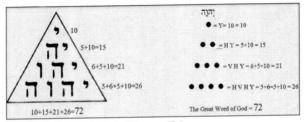

Figure 76

Immediately I emailed back, asking who they were and why they were contacting me. Unfortunately there was no response, but I assumed that it must have had something to do with all the information I had let loose on the pen drive; most likely the mysterious source had decided to make contact.

As I stared at the face of Enoch's Stone on screen, I started to realise just how deep the mathematical code went regarding the Lost Word, since when the Name of God was triangulated, and each letter assigned its traditional Hebraic numerological value, it did indeed equate to 72, the number of angelic names in the Lost Word. It was as if the Hebrew alphabet had been constructed with this one idea in mind. Or was it that the construct of the 'written word' had somehow been part of the master plan, the plan of the Immortal Man of Light? As requested, I also turned to the Gnostic story and discovered that the mysterious source was absolutely right. A fundamental aspect of the story was about how the mortal, Adam, was to be created. And the only way to do this was by somehow enclosing or containing the divine light.

Of course I did watch the three episodes of *The Code* and it took me deeper still, to a place that I would never have gone. It explained how we can use the thing we call 'number' to decode the underlying principles that governed the universe. By using rational, irrational and transcendental numbers, or the numbers used to create the geometric triad – the square, triangle and circle or Philosophers' Stone – the expression of the Great Architect in us can be defined. Moreover, as part of the professor's 'Code' there is also a geo-numeric element that can be found in nature to describe how the world was created.

The message here was that the rules or laws governing the evolution of the geological world, and the evolution of all species, are based in geometry. And that these so-called 'fractal geo-numeric rules' can be found not only in the visible world, but also in the very substance that is used to make us, DNA.

I was at last starting to see some of the deepest elements of the mystery, the hidden knowledge in us, the true nature of the intelligent design of the Grand Architect; knowledge that had been understood at varying levels and passed down through the ages by secret fraternities. But how would this help me to resolve the mystery? Would knowledge of this 'divine' code somehow help to provide the means by which to complete the quest to regain Paradise? Would the answer come to me in a dream? Or was this the final level of the mystery? How could there be another level? As I saw it, the only level left would have to reside in some sort of spiritual or religious experience, like that of Enoch meeting with angels, or Solomon conversing with God Himself. But I knew that something like this could never really happen.

A few days later I accessed my email account to make contact with Robin. Again, I had an unexpected message, "Have You Cracked the Code?" I replied immediately, "Jehovah, light, intelligent design and no solution. Thanks for the Enigma Machine. No miracle witnessed as yet." I left it for a few minutes and to my surprise another email arrived, "I will phone you in five". Seconds later the phone rang. I jumped up to answer it.

"Hello."

The reply came back in a broad Yorkshire accent, but with some sort of foreign twist, Spanish, perhaps Italian, and I somehow recognised the woman's voice.

"Are you aware that you are not the only one?"

"Only one what?"

"The only one to have discovered the secret. But what intrigues me most is that you have discovered many strands of the mystery that have alluded, let's say, prominent people who have invested a lot of time and resources into progressing this project."

"So other people know about the quest to regain Paradise? Anyway, who are you? Did you make the machine? Your voice sounds familiar."

"No, not me, I don't possess such skills, but I saw a version of it once, possibly the original, in a private collection. A little less complicated than the Antikythera mechanism, with its angelic 72 gears,[8] but quite obviously a lot older."

"The Anti what mechanism?"

"This mechanism, alongside other versions, was built to calculate the timing of the quest, the Procession of the Ages, when the prophesy will be fulfilled."

"So how did you get my contact details?"

"When you blatantly scattered such important information to the wind, the smell was picked up by many different beasts. How such news spreads like wild fire. Do you know of the concept of six degrees of separation?"

"I'm just two away from Kylie Minogue as it happens."

"Yes, the idea that everyone is on average approximately six steps away, by introduction, to any other person on earth. I would hazard a guess that the knowledgeable gentleman that provided you with the machine is around four from you."

"So who are you?"

"Let's just say that I have a vested interest in seeing if you can help discover how to see beyond the light. You are still missing a few important pieces, which I can give to you, but I cannot show you the way, I can only guide you to the veil. How it is to be drawn aside I do not know. But I do know that it has to be done. *Mente videbor*, 'by the mind I shall be seen'."

"This is all some sort of joke, right?"

"Whether you want to believe it or not, there are many waiting, poised, on the side-lines, watching the game that has no boundaries, the game that spans all history. As I have already stated, you seem to see things in a different light and I would be happy to help you see a little more. What do you think, no strings attached?"

"OK, I'll play along for now. I've nothing to lose, I suppose."

There was a long pause.

"Get yourself a pen and paper."

"No need. I always switch on my digital recorder when I have an important call."

"The following will set you off. And remember, it is sometimes the journey, not the arriving. Many people may tread the same path, acquiring knowledge that they believe is junk, but to others it is treasure. I read your treatise with great interest and know you understand just how the path to enlightenment has to be navigated. So, written into the complex iconography that exists in the Chapter House are several hidden symbols that depict just what it does, what it is, a portal that will lead to the light."

"You don't say."

"In the original Pyramid Texts, which eventually inspired the *Book of Emerging forth into the Light*, there is a description of the original spells or utterances that would enable the candidate, the pharaoh in this case, to safely navigate his way to the celestial realm. If you look carefully at the array of splendid carvings that surround the walls of the Chapter House, you can piece together most of the utterances. For example, the Opening of the Mouth Ceremony is easily picked out, and the bodily gifts that would enable the candidate to face the nine great gods, the Ennead, are very prominent. I have just sent you an email with words from the utterances and two of the corresponding images from the Chapter House."

I checked my inbox and it was there. I opened it and clicked on the attachment (fig. 77), and then read the accompanying words as the woman waited in silence:

I have given to thee the eye of Horus, so that thy face may be equipped; the white teeth of Horus which equip thy mouth, and thy nose, that of Anubis,

imperishable. With that wherewith he opened the mouth that he himself may speak before the Great Ennead.[9]

Figure 77

"OK. I see it. The famous Toothache Man from the Chapter House. He is about to speak with the Ennead. So, whoever named him did not understand his meaning."

"Not necessarily. You see, in the Gnostic art of tarot, the candidate is depicted not as the pharaoh, but as the Fool, the Gnostic agent. And in many decks, such as the Tarot of Marseilles, the Fool is depicted wearing the Fool's cap."

"Foolscap paper, the hidden gnostic watermark, the Fool."

"That's right. And the Fool's card traditionally had no number. But Eliphas Levi, the great occultist, assigned not a number, but a Hebrew letter to the Fool's card, the letter *Shin*, meaning 'tooth',[10] the Toothache Man. He placed it between the two final cards in tarot; twenty, 'Judgment' and twenty-one, the final card in tarot, 'The World'. Of course, the Gnostic agent here stands between Judgement and the World. And in the end this is exactly what someone will have to do."

"The judgment of the world?"

"The Opening of the Mouth Ceremony has become something of a symbol for those who have been privy to the quest throughout the ages. It has also been rendered into many cultural traditions, such as the Mori haka or Manawa wera, where the opening of the mouth and sticking out of the tongue is used to symbolise the final funerary challenge to the gods, for the right to access the celestial realm. And just like much of the symbolism relating to the quest that has become part of the Fool's tradition, the Opening of the Mouth, to the untrained eye, is now perceived as a comical gesture. But its origins arc back to the final case that the candidate has to be put before the gods, the Ennead."

"So this ceremony is all about the candidate presenting their case to the Ennead, about the Authority's right to rule in Paradise?"

"All but a few thought that Einstein was pulling out his tongue to the reporters on his birthday. But he had specifically waited for his 72nd birthday[11] to send out the message of the Opening of the Mouth."

"The angelic essence, 72?"

Another email suddenly arrived and I clicked on the attached image (fig. 78).

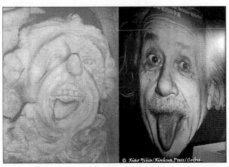

Figure 78

"That's uncanny. So is this carving in the Chapter House?"

"Yes. But what is most interesting is that Einstein also added to the message. He asked for a very specific number of copies of this iconic image to be sent to him."

"What, 72?"

"Try again and think not of the number of angelic names or the Lost Word, but of the end game, when the candidate's mouth is opened to the gods."

"Nine. The Ennead?"

"That's right, nine, he specifically asked for nine copies."[12]

"All this is just a coincidence though, isn't it?"

"In June, 2009 one of the nine photographs, which was signed by Einstein, was sold at auction. He wrote a message on this particular photograph. Would you like to know what it says?"

"Well, if it has anything to do with the salvation of the human race and the quest to regain Paradise, I will eat my hat."

"The inscription reads: 'This gesture you will like, because it is aimed at all of humanity'."[13]

"OK. Let's say you are telling me the truth. You said that there were other things. What are they?"

"I will contact you again tomorrow and tell you a little more. It's been a pleasure. I hope I have not made a mistake."

"So do I."

13th Degree

The Stone of Destiny

It felt as if I was trapped in a Dan Brown novel, but at the same time stuck in the world of Harry Potter, with a twist of Indiana Jones thrown in, all surrounded by the construct of the *Matrix*. But it was all real, real life. And where would it end? Where would the rabbit hole finally take me? George had been right. It had been a dangerous game to play. It had consumed over two decades of my life. I was a Leo, and I had just turned forty years old. Memento mori.

The Secret of Poor Robin's Intelligence

Early the next morning I was awoken by the telephone. I leant across and picked it up.

"Hello."

"It's me. Do you know Robin Hood's Well on the Great North Road?"

"I know it well. It's at the heart of Barnsdale, my favourite place in the world. My dad always took…"

"Would you meet me there around 10am?"

"No problem. It's been a long time and it looks like it's going to be a nice day."

"I'll see you there then. Oh, and would you bring the introduction to *New Atlantis* with you, the one that was sent to you by Thomas, the Rosicrucian adept?"

"Of course."

The sun was shining and the familiar drive south to Barnsdale was extremely pleasant. When I arrived, I pulled into the lay-by next to Robin Hood's Well and immediately saw a figure crouched down, back resting against the well. As I got out of the car the figure rose up and began waving. I waved back and moved towards the well. As I got closer I saw a beautiful smile, perfect lips curling strangely upwards, then the raggle-taggle-type gypsy dress with a few little flecks of silver and coloured beads dripping from its midpoint and underarms. She looked as if she was in her mid-thirties, with delicately curled, ebony-coloured hair that stood firm, yet bounced beside her olive coloured face. As I approached I held out my hand. She half took hold of it, covered it with her other hand and then pressed firmly with her thumb onto my knuckles. I had thought of something nice to say, but it didn't quite come out as I had hoped.

"I thought you would be much older, a pleasure to meet you. By the way, I love your accent."

"It's a complicated one. Pleased to meet you too."

She turned and leant against the well, playfully tapping her hands against it. I had my digital recorder on a leather bootlace around my neck. I pointed to it.

"Do you mind if I switch this on, I have a terrible memory?"

"No, not at all. So, why do you think that Robin Hood survived through the ages, his legend now known to millions, no, billions of people across the globe?"

"I suppose he is the personification of the eternal archer, Apollo, ever present, letting loose his arrows of light into the murky shadows, the places where evil and injustice attempt to hide. He is the undying, mystical hero of the common man, and woman of course."

"I like that. Well put and politically correct. Or could it be that there is more to his story than meets the eye. Just like Lewis Carroll's White Rabbit, could it be that Robin Hood has been preserved throughout the ages because he is the icon for an important secret; preserved in the mysterious ballads, mystery plays and legends that were brought to life by minstrels, gleemen, troubadours, jogelers, jesters and gypsies. Maybe the secret was not necessarily about the character Robin Hood, but the events surrounding the life of the man behind the myth."

"But no one knows who Robin Hood was, do they? Anyway, before we get into this, tell me about you, and there are others?"

"Did you know that in the early ballads and stories that talk about Robin Hood, his name is actually spelt differently, not 'Robin Hood', but 'Robin Hode'. In fact this spelling was used up until at least the 16th century."[1]

"So, about you then?"

She laughed for a long moment.

"I have a story to tell. Would you like to hear it?"

"Of course."

"It is a true story about a man that lived in the 17th century called Henry Care, who once tried to unravel the secret of Poor Robin's Intelligence.[2] Mr Henry Care was a professional writer based in London. He wrote about lots of things, from the achievements of notable women, to various medical remedies available at the time. One day, while in his office, in the year 1676, he was called-on by an elderly gentleman who told him that certain members of a society in Edinburgh were the keepers of a secret of such importance that it was unthinkable that it could be lost to time."

"A very important secret then?"

"He explained to Henry that he had a document in his possession which could compromise this secret, and that it was imperative he passed it on to someone in case he met his demise. The gentleman gave Henry a package, headed with a note that read, 'Robin Hode is key, do not forget Poor Robin's Intelligence.' He then explained to Henry that he would contact him again in a couple of months, and left."

"So what was in the package?"

"After opening the package Henry found a small piece of vellum with just a few words written on it."

"Which were?"

"It said 'Robin Hode', then a hyphen, and then, with a capitalised G, an old spelling of the name for Edinburgh Town, 'EdinboroGh'.[3] I must also explain that this particular spelling was used by Thomas d'Urfey, who wrote the words for the song *Within a Furlong of Edinborogh Town*. As I recall it goes something like, 'Twas within a furlong of Edinborogh Town, in the rosy time of year'. There was of course a certain Rosicrucian influence at play here."

"You mean the Rosy Cross?"

"Henry obviously wanted to know more about the secret of Poor Robin's Intelligence and, more specifically, why he had been chosen to hold on to it. After a few months the gentleman did not return, so Henry decided to produce a satirical news sheet, acting as a provocative means by which to, hopefully, coax the gentleman to return. In a clever move he headed his newssheet *Poor Robin's Intelligence.* As it happens the newssheet took-off and became rather popular, but the man never got back in contact."

"So what happened next?"

"Have you got that copy of the introduction to *New Atlantis* on you? When I first saw it in your work I could not believe my eyes."

"I have brought the original. It's a little bigger than the cropped example in my work."

I took it out of my leather satchel and gave it to her (fig. 79).

"Look here, see, 'Edinborogh' with the capitalised 'G'."

I looked closely.

"You're right. I had never noticed it before. So what does it mean?"

"It can mean many things, but in secret societies the capitalised 'G' is usually used to denote the Great Architect. I have examples if you would like to see them."

Figure 79

"No, that's alright, I have seen the 'G' symbol on Masonic tracing boards and once at the heart of a pentacle on a Masonic gravestone in Kendal churchyard."

"Also, look at the strange symbols at the top right hand corner."

I dipped into my satchel again, pushed aside my camera and compass, took hold of my small magnifying glass and focussed in on the symbols (fig. 80).

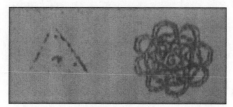

Figure 80

"It looks like a triangle with an eye inside, the all-seeing eye of God. And the Ogdoad symbol, with the capitalised 'G' at the centre."

"So, in the word 'EdinboroGh', which would you say is the odd letter out?"

"Well, if it's not a trick question, then I would say the letter 'G'."

She passed me a piece of paper.

"I have moved out the 'G'. Now rearrange the remaining letters and tell me what you see."

I could clearly see the 'G' moved over to one side and the remaining letters, 'edinboroh'. Swapping the letters around in my mind, it suddenly came to me. I could not believe it.

"That's great; it's an anagram. The remaining letters rearranged spell 'Robin Hode'. That's fantastic."

She passed me another piece of paper.

"Many people have suggested that the mind behind the works of Shakespeare belonged to the Rosicrucian Grand Master, Francis Bacon, and that he encoded many Rosicrucian ciphers into them."

"Really?"

"Yes it's a well-established theory."[4]

"And your point is?"

"Look at the words on the paper. They come from Act 1, Scene 1 of Shakespeare's or perhaps Bacon's *Richard III*. Apart from the obvious Rosy Cross or should I say cross row influence, look at what the wizard proposed."

I read the words:

He hearkens after prophecies and dreams;
And from the cross-row plucks the letter G.
And says a wizard told him that by G
His issue disinherited should be.

I smiled.

"So this is basically the cypher for decoding the secret of Poor Robin's Intelligence. But still, what does it mean? Is there something in Edinburgh, Bacon's Rosicrucian College, Solomon's House perhaps? And why Robin Hood? And by the way, here we are unravelling some of the most profound mysteries of the ages and I don't even know your name."

"My friends call me Lily, but I am really called Lilith."

"So may I call you Lily?"

She again ignored my feeble attempt to draw her into a personal conversation.

"You are right, to an extent. An important branch of Bacon's college, Solomon's House, resided just to the south of Edinburgh, only slightly more than a furlong shall we say. But before we speak of this, I first need to explain who Robin Hode really was. The pieces will then be easier to fit together."

"I'm all ears."

"The very earliest stories and ballads that talk about Robin Hode put him right here in the once centre of the Ancient Forest of Barnsdale, on the site of his well.[5] And the name 'Robin' was originally a diminutive given name for Robert; and *Hode*, his second name, was chosen since it meant 'hide' in Anglo-Saxon. And so the name was created, as a code, to hide and safeguard the identity of a powerful Robert from Barnsdale that once hid or protected something of great importance."

"What?"

"Robert de Lacy was descended from French stock, and in the 12th century he held several vast estates, one of which encompassed the whole of Barnsdale, places such as Skelbrooke and Skellow, where the Chief Druid lived, Godfrey Higgins."

"So Higgins knew about this?"

"In the 16th century story about the antics of Robin Hode, the playwright Anthony Munday goes into detail about the Lacy family and wittingly implies that Robert de Lacy, as Robert Earl of Huntington,[6] Huntington in York that is, was Robin Hode. He explains how he married a Matilda and was banished for a short while, which corresponds directly to historical events.[7] More so, according to the *Little Geste of Robin Hode*, the earliest known story about Robin, it talks of a chapel that he built in Barnsdale."[8]

"A chapel?"

"Yes, in both the story and historical records it specifically states that this chapel, in Skelbrooke, was affiliated to the Priory of St. Mary Magdalene in Bretton, also in Yorkshire.[9] The Bretton coat of arms, Archangel Michael holding a shield with three covered chalices, can still be seen on this very chapel that was built by Robert de Lacy,[10] or Robin Hode as stated in the story. And then there is the Earl of Chest..."

"Hold on. What was he protecting?"

"The only thing that would give a mortal access to Paradise, the one thing that could be built into a temple; the corner stone, the cornerstone that the other builders had to reject."

"Cornerstone?"

"Yes, the very stone that was built into the Chapter House, as part of the prophesy."

"But what stone could give us access to Paradise?"

"Silly, Jacob's Pillar, the stone that Jacob used as a pillow to access the celestial realm."

Lily took out a laptop from her bag that was leaning against the well. She opened it up and it immediately came to life. After a few clicks she turned the screen towards me (fig. 81).

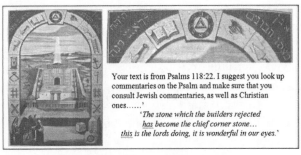

Figure 81

"This is a tracing board for the Mark Master Mason Degree. It shows what will eventually happen when the stone performs its function in the temple. Notice the light emitting from the dome that covers the octagonal form. You might also want to read the translation of the Hebrew I acquired, which is written on the tracing board. The board is depicting a vision of the final temple."

"Wait a minute. Are you saying that Jacob's Pillar was somehow passed down through time to eventually come into the hands of Robin Hood, Robert de Lacy, and that this is why the legend of Robin Hood has been preserved over the ages?"

"Robert de Lacy eventually took up residence at one of his priories on the outskirts of Barnsdale, Nostell Priory.[11] And after some debate with King Alexander I of Scotland, it was decided that Robert and his head canon would found the Royal Monastery of Scone in Scotland. [12] This is why Nostell Priory became the Mother House to Scone."

"So a small Yorkshire priory on the outskirts of Barnsdale became the Mother House to a royal monastery in Scone. So what has this got to do with anything?"

"Scone, Scone."

As she said the place name for the second time it came to me.

"Scone. The Stone of Scone, the Stone of Destiny."

"Ah, you see it now."

"I know this legend. The Stone of Destiny, which I believe resides in the Crown Room at Edinburgh Castle, is said to be the very stone that..."

"Jacob used to access the celestial realm..."

"Jacob's Pillar. This is major. Can you prove all this?"

"It is a fact. That is, the link between Robert de Lacy, Nostell Priory, Scone and Jacob's Pillar. Of course the idea that the stone in Edinburgh is Jacob's pillar is based on quite a complicated legend. At least that's what the guard at the Crown Room explained to me. There were many copies of the stone made. I know for sure that the one at Edinburgh is a copy. Also the one that was kept by Chevalier Reverend John Mackay at the Church of St. Columba in Dundee was a fake. Such replicas were used to protect the original in times of conflict. The real one of course, the corner stone that had to be rejected over the ages, was built into the Chapter House by King Edward I, Longshanks."

"So why was it rejected by these so called other builders?"

"You know this. As part of the prophesy it had to be built into the temple at Eborakon, the Place of the Tree of Life, its prophesised resting place; the epicentre of the original and New Jerusalem."

"And Edward I?"

"When the Stone of Destiny was taken from Nostell to Scone, and Robert died, it remained there until the English king, Edward, took it back using force, in 1296. He then, under written instruction from his departed Uncle, Frederick II, the once King of Jerusalem and Emperor of the Holy Roman Empire, had it built into the Chapter House, in 1298."

"He built it into the Chapter House?"

"He also took one of the fake stones from Scone, and it has been used since then by every English monarch, as a seat, on which to be crowned, just like it was used by all the High Kings of Tara in Ireland."

"So every monarch including the current queen has been crowned upon a fake Jacob's Pillar since Edward's time?"

"That's right. It was a latter addition to the prophesy. But, ironically, a thousand years of English monarchs did not know it was a fake. I suppose that's a story in itself."

"So why did Edward do it?"

"We can talk a little bit more about Edward's role when we look at the final part of the mystery. I realise now that you never thought to check the stained glass in the Chapter House, did you?"

"Yes, you're right, I did not. What's in it? And what's the story behind Jacob's Pillar? How did it get from Bethel in the Holy Land to here?

"It's an extremely fascinating story. I suppose you want to hear it?"

"What do you think?"

Jacobs Pillar

My mind was racing. If what Lily was proposing was true, it would at last explain how the temple, the Chapter House, could act as a portal or nexus between this world and the celestial realm.

She placed her hand on my shoulder.

"Would you like to continue this in a more pleasant spot, down at Skelbrooke perhaps, next to the chapel from the story?"

"Yes, that would be nice."

Strangely, few words were passed as we made our way down to the ancient chapel. Once there we picked a turfy spot, Lily took out a trendy looking flask of coffee, poured out a generous helping and took a small drink. She then offered me the cup, opened up her laptop and began her intriguing lecture.

"In 1249 Alexander was crowned Scottish King, Alexander III, at Scone, Scotland. And it is recorded that on the crown touching his head a veteran, kilted Highlander recited the new King's royal decendancy through fifty-six generations; from King Fergus I, back to Scota, daughter of Pharaoh, King of Egypt."[13]

"Scottish royalty were descended from Egyptian blood? Has this got something to do with the Stone then?"

"This is how Scotland gained its name, from Princess Scotia."

"Interesting."

"Now, if we go back to the beginning, basically the Irish and Scottish legends[14] explain that, after his divine experience with the stone, Jacob kept it as a prized possession until the time when it was taken into Egypt with the Twelve Tribes of Israel. Eventually Jacob died, leaving an increasing Israelite population in Egypt; and with the appointment of a new Pharaoh the Israelites were enslaved."

"Basically the beginnings of the *Exodus* story then?"

"Jacob had a special son called Judah, who had a son called Zerah, who in turn had a son called Calcol, who became the leader of a band of Israelites that fled from Egypt and founded Athens in BC 1556.[15] While ruling Athens, Calcol had a son called Gathelus Miledh, who eventually sailed back to Egypt in a time of strife, in order to help the Pharaoh in battle, so that he might free his people."

Scrolling down the screen, Lily continued with confidence.

"Gathelus Miledh then spent seven years in Egypt, and in turn gained the hand in marriage of Princess Scota, daughter of the Pharaoh of Egypt. While there, Gathelus Miledh moved among his captive, Israelite brethren, and with instructions from Moses took Jacob's Pillar and left with a large contingent of the Twelve Tribes of Israel, eventually reaching Brigantia on the northern border between Portugal and Spain."

"The Tribes of Israel went to Spain?"

"After a major battle in Spain, Gathelus Miledh crafted a coronation chair, in which the stone became the seat."

"So it was now part of a chair?"

"Yes. And in Andrew of Wyntoun's *Orygynale Chronicle* of 1420,[16] he similarly describes the stone as part of a chair or throne that was in Spain before it came to Britain."

"I suppose it could be easily hidden in a chair?"

"No. The stone was much bigger than that. It formed the seat from the ground up."

"A hefty thing then."

"In an ancient text called *The Book of the Taking of Ireland* or *Leabhar Gabhala* and other similar legends,[17] Gathelus Miledh and the Egyptian princess, Scotia, had a son called Erimhon. Here Erimhon married Ith's daughter, who was called Tea or Teah-Tephi; and when Gathelus Miledh died, Ith made a journey to Ireland and was killed by the Irish forces. When news of this reached Spain, a small army made up of the Tribes of Israel set out with Scotia and Teah-Tephi to conquer the land."

"The Tribes of Israel went to Ireland?"

"From the *Annals of the Kingdom of Ireland*[18] we hear that Tea-Tephi requested from her husband, Erimhon, a piece of land that she might call her own, and in later times be buried. The place she selected was Teamhair of Tara, in Ireland, where her tomb is now said to reside. From this site, which was renamed Brigantia, after the tribes' distant homeland in Spain, all the kings of Scotia Major or Ireland were said to be crowned upon the chair. This went on for well over a thousand years, and around AD 500, King Erc was chronicled as the High-King at Tara. At this point we hear about the next movement of the chair, from Tara in Ireland to Scotland, which became known as Scotia Minor."

"So now the Stone has reached Scotland?"

"In Hector Boece's *Chronicles of Scotland*[19] it specifically states that Fergus, son of King Erc, was the first King of the Scots in Scotland, and that he brought the chair, which held within it Jacob's Pillar, from Ireland to Argyll, and was crowned upon it at the summit fortress of Dunadd."

Lily looked as if she was in a trance. She opened up another file.

"Fergus then built a church at Iona, just off the western shores of Scotland, and commanded it to be the sepulchre of future kings. The chair was housed for a while at Iona, and then moved to Dunstaffnage Castle on mainland Scotland, under the protection of the MacDougal clan. Interestingly, in the year 1833, Captain Campbell of Inistore was given permission to exhibit a curious and interesting relic to a select group of people."[20]

"What sort of relic?"

"An ancient, ivory chess piece from the ruins of Dunstaffnage Castle, depicting the crowned monarch sitting on a chair, in which Jacob's Pillar made up its seat."

Lily turned the screen towards me (fig. 82).

"Wow, that's the stone as the seat?"

"In the mid-800s, Kenneth MacAlpin was crowned as the first King of the united kingdom of the Picts and the Scots, upon the chair; and once crowned he founded a small church at Scone, where the chair apparently resided."

"Apparently resided?"

"Well, you do know of another place that was named Brigantia at the time of the movement of the chair from Spain, don't you?"

Figure 82

"Of course, Brigantia, Yorkshire. Are you saying that members of the Tribes of Israel brought the real chair to Yorkshire, to the prophesised New Jerusalem?"

"It is of course not written, but there are some who believe that the chair was actually taken to a place near here."

"What, Nostell Priory?"

"When Robert de Lacy founded the royal monastery at Scone, for a reason that no one knows, it is believed that he took it there. That is, until it was forcibly removed by Edward I." Lily stood up and packed her things away. "Come on, I'll take you to see the real Robin Hood's Well."

As we walked across the top of a familiar quarry, toward the main road, Lily began explaining about another well in Barnsdale.

"The original Robin Hood's Well was moved when the current well, designed by the famous architect Sir

John Vanbrugh, was erected. Before the new well was put in place it had been visited by many notable people including the French Prince and poet, the Duke of Orleans and Margaret Tudor. But the most significant visit was in 1654 by the diarist John Evelyn, a member of the Rosicrucian Order, Invisible College, and one of the founding members of the Royal Society. That is, the society that was dedicated to pursuing the goals of the once Rosicrucian Master..."

"Francis Bacon. Yes I know of this."

"Evelyn describes the well as having a stone chair with an iron ladle attached to it.[21] This stone chair was moved to another spring when the new well was erected."

"What, you mean Little John's Well?"

"Yes, you can even make out the two lead filled holes that were used to secure the chain for the ladle."

As we approached the well I could clearly see the back of what looked like a stone chair, but no seat; no stone. Was Lily going to suggest something completely radical? Could this be the chair that once housed Jacob's Pillar? A chair at a well dedicated to the man that had founded the Royal Monastery of Scone; Robert de Lacy, the man behind the myth of Robin Hood (Fig. 83).

Figure 83

Lily again booted up her laptop and quickly found what she was looking for.

"I'm not saying that this is the chair that was crafted in Spain, but it may be. When I was asked to investigate the chair back, I acquired the exact measurements of Jacobs Pillar, from the copy in the Crown Room at Edinburgh Castle. It measures 670mm long, 420mm wide and 265mm deep. I then measured the chair back and drew them out to see if it was a match. As I drew it out, it seemed that the ledge on the chair back acted as a natural top support to complete the chair, very similar to the chair that held the fake stone in Westminster Abbey for all those years." (Fig. 84).

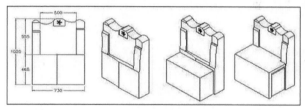

Figure 84

"Chair at Westminster Abbey?"

"The one used to crown all the British Monarchs."

"Oh, yes."

"I also contacted a Professor from the Hunterian Museum at Glasgow University, where several alter-type chairs of antiquity can also be found. I emailed him what I had discovered and he said that he had not seen anything like it before, and that it was one of a kind."

As I looked at her drawings on screen, I was starting to realise that I had indeed been caught up in something that was much bigger than I had originally thought. Lily turned to me.

"That didn't take long now, did it? So what next? Let me think. I need to explain how the Tree of Life managed to find its way to the Chapter House as well. Are you game?"

"Undoubtedly."

"I will contact you in a couple of days."

With this she made her way to a car with someone in the passenger side, which was parked in the lay-by, just down from the well.

14th Degree

The Tree of Life

On the verge of devising a profound ending for my journey of discovery, I was in two minds whether to contact Robin Wade. There were still so many questions to be asked, so many questions to be answered. Was there a network of people caught up in this profound mystery? Who was the driving force behind Lily? Had she been caught up in this just like me, a pawn in a much larger game? Or was she actually a member of some sort of syndicate, a modern day group, society or fraternity that was responsible for secretly preserving the elements of the quest to regain Paradise? Moreover, was there in fact a way to complete the quest, to fulfil the prophesy? One thing was for sure, I would not stop until I had found out.

And I in Arcadia

It was around two days later when I received an email from Lily, asking to meet me again at Robin Hood's Well. It was raining this time, but I did not care since the journey south was just as refreshing.

As I turned into the lay-by I could see Lily in the passenger seat of her large, powerful, five series BMW. I pulled up behind her and got out. I could see through the back window that she was beavering away on her laptop. As I approached the passenger side door she looked up and smiled, while beckoning me to go round to the driver's side. I did as she asked, and once inside she immediately placed a finger on her lips and continued reading from the text on screen. A few moments later she slapped down the screen.

"You drive."

"Where to?"

"I've inputted it into the Sat Nav. I need to get some shuteye, I've been awake all night preparing. Wake me up when we get there."

"Where?"

"Shugborough, Shugborough Hall."

Having driven an automatic car before, I put it into 'drive' and we were off. In between wrestling with the lights and windscreen wipers, the journey was very comfortable. I believe my eyes must have spent more time on the sleeping beauty than that of the grey road ahead. Once we arrived at Shugborough, I parked the car and placed my hand on her shoulder, gently nudging her awake. Her large brown eyes were suddenly staring at me. She smiled, sat up, stretched and reopened the laptop she had been hugging throughout the journey. She placed it on the central armrest.

"This is the internet site for Shugborough Hall."

She began reading from the Homepage.

"Can you crack the code? Do you have what it takes to solve one of the most mystifying secrets in natural history? The code sits beneath a marble relief in the gardens of this ancestral home."

"Another code, eh?"

"Unfortunately for everyone, the code does not sit beneath the marble relief, as they suggest, it is actually contained within the marble relief itself. Did you know that in 2004 Shugborough invited World War II code breakers from Bletchley Park to look into the code? Ironic don't you think?"

"So what's the code about then?"

"Well, let's take a look."

We exited the car and it seemed that Lily knew exactly where she was going. After about five minutes we were in some sort of small garden, facing a strange stone monument of sorts, protected by a roof that was supported by two weird looking columns. As we approached the monument Lily pointed to the central scene (fig. 85).

Figure 85

"Rumour has it that the Shugborough monument is hiding a set of instructions on how to find the Holy Grail."

"The Holy Grail? What has this to do with anything?"

"Over the years, both professional code-breakers and the general public have been invited to crack this code but have never been successful. The monument also appears in a couple of best-selling books written about the Holy

Grail. The inset marble scene is an inverse or mirror image of a painting by the 17th century artist, Nicolas Poussin. I believe the painting is held at the Louvre in Paris, entitled, *Les bergers d'Arcadie*."

"Which means?"

"The Arcadian shepherds. Of course, just like the differences on the *Tempest* text on the Shakespeare Monument at Westminster Abbey, the marble depiction here at Shugborough Hall is slightly different to Poussin's original painting."

"The *Tempest* text."

"Yes, Shakespeare is pointing to Solomon's Temple in the text. A solemn gesture I think."

"So when are you going to tell me how you know all this stuff. And what about the others involved with the quest? I saw someone in your car."

"When the time is right I will tell you everything. Can you agree to this? If not, this all ends now."

"Whatever you say."

"The original, allegorical meaning of this shepherd scene is quite complex, and a pseudo-history has been attached to the Shugborough copy over the years. The additional Latin inscription under the monument is said to be a code that will reveal the resting place of the Grail."

"But the Grail, what does it have..."

"Just listen. Unfortunately for the code-breakers and conspiracy theorists, the Latin inscription is a red herring of sorts. To a great extent, people have simply been looking in the wrong place. When I first saw the Shugborough Monument, it was plainly obvious that the code was contained in the letters which the Shepherds are pointing to."

"What, the words written on the Tomb?"

"Before I show you what it says, you must think back to the time when the painting of this scene took place."

"In the time of Rosicrucian enlightenment, Francis Bacon's time?"

"Exactly. So with Bacon in mind, see if you can crack this un-crackable code."

As I looked carefully at the scene, I noticed that the Arcadian shepherds were pointing to specific letters, using both fingers and thumbs. And even though the middle parts of the fingers were broken away, the tips still remained. I could see that one thumb was forming what looked like a letter 'B', the tip of one finger was resting on the letter 'N' and another seemed to be hovering above the letter 'C'. I looked to the remaining letters, 'A' and 'O'.

"Have you worked it out yet?"

"I don't believe it, another anagram, 'BACON', the Rosicrucian Grand Master, Francis Bacon."

Unflustered by this, Lily continued.

"The full Latin text on the monument translates to 'And I in Arcadia'."

"And I in Arcadia? What Francis Bacon was in Arcadia?"

Figure 86

"He was the guiding father of the colonisation scheme, misguided however."

She paused for a moment and squinted.

"The Romans took the word 'Arcadia' from the first Greeks, who used it to describe a forested hilly terrain in the Greek Peloponnese. The word 'Arcadia' then took on the poetical meaning, still used today as a metaphor for rural simplicity; the traditional life enjoyed by shepherds in the countryside. If you look at the scene, you can see that the image is capturing a moment when the shepherds' state of bliss has come to an end."

"Come to an end?"

"According to art-experts, the scene is depicting a moment of revelation, when an unknown woman unveils an ancient tomb with an inscription that holds some sort of deep and serious implication for the shepherds."

"Like what?"

"In the early 1980s, the writers Baigent, Leigh, and Lincoln, in their ground-breaking book, *The Holy Blood and the Holy Grail*, made an attempt to link the tomb depicted on Poussin's painting and the Shugborough Monument to a similar looking construction that existed just a short way from the famous Grail church at Rennes le Château in southern France."

"Interesting."

"Pseudo-historians have since jumped on the bandwagon, adding to the claim that the tomb held the body of Jesus, Mary Magdalene, or one of their royal blood descendants. You know, *The Da Vinci Code*?"

"I never read it, but I know about the idea, sort of. I spoke to a man called Laurence Gardner about it years ago. He was very helpful, but I believe he has now passed away."

"You spoke to Gardner?"

"Yes, at length, several times. Problem?"

"No, but that might explain a few things."

"Like what?"

"When I visited Rennes le Château I did find something of interest. But it was only when I visited the Rosslyn Grail chapel just to the south of Edinburgh that things started to fall into place."

"Back to Robin Hood then."

"Yes, about ten feet away from the Apprentice Pillar I again found a reference to Arcadia."

"Apprentice pillar?"

"The stone column that some say holds the Grail."

"And the Arcadia link?"

She began clicking on her laptop and then turned it towards me (fig. 87).

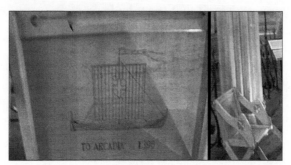

Figure 87

"As you can see, on the back of one of the chapel's chairs is the words 'To Arcadia', accompanied by a depiction of a sailing ship with the engrailed cross of the Sinclair family of Rosslyn, on its way to Arcadia in 1398. So why do you think members of the Sinclair family would want to travel to Arcadia in 1398? But more interestingly, why would the chapel want to commemorate such a journey?"

"I assume you are going to tell me."

"In 1398 Prince Henry Sinclair visited Arcadia, but not the Arcadia in the Greek Peloponnese, the one that is now referred to as New Scotland or Nova Scotia, Canada." [1]

"So you are saying that the word Arcadia on this monument, Poussin's original painting and the chair at the Rosslyn Grail chapel all link to a mystery surrounding the Holy Grail and Nova Scotia, New Scotland."

"Yes and no really. Yes the Grail, but not as you or anyone else knows it."

"You've lost me."

"Don't worry, all will be revealed, just be patient. In early medieval times, a turbulent time in the quest to regain Paradise's history, many interpretations of the prophesy were put forward. There was the French version, which had it that Jerusalem in the Holy Land would become the New Jerusalem, and that the temple would be built on the same site as the old temple."

"Solomon's Temple?"

"Yes. And then there was the British schism between two powerful groups of guardians. Basically, another hypothesis or interpretation of the prophesy was put forward, which ultimately influenced Francis Bacon to create his democratic blueprint for the New Atlantis, the New Jerusalem."

"New Atlantis is another name for the New Jerusalem?"

"Early on though, this new interpretation had struck a chord with the powerful Washington Knights that lived in Barnsdale, after the Lacy family. It was proposed that the final temple should be built on a land that had been discovered many, many years before it was officially discovered."

"What, Arcadia, Newfoundland?"

"Yes. But it did not quite work out as planned. And it was eventually decided by Francis Bacon that the temple would be built just down from Nova Scotia. So a plan was put in place and the colonisation process began, across the Atlantic, to what would in effect become the New Jerusalem. Ultimately this led to a secret war that was masked by a fight for independence."[2]

"You mean the War of Independence?"

"Still, a Washington was chosen, raised to power and inaugurated as the first President of the United States."

"So George Washington's ancestors lived in Barnsdale?"

"Yes, a branch of the Rosicrucian Washington's; they were holders of the secret of Poor Robin's Intelligence after the Lacy dynasty." [3]

"I'm sure I read something about this."

"Yes, Robert Lomas, in his *Turning the Solomon Key*, dealt with the idea that Washington was obsessed with creating a Masonic Capital of the world, and that he was, for various reasons, infatuated with Venus."

"Venus. The Venus prophesy?"

"But only you, I and a few select others are privy to Washington's true motivations."

"So where was the new temple built."

"It was never really built."

"OK. So where was it going to be built?"

"They renamed the place New York."

"New York?" It came to me in a sudden rush. "New York, New Eborakon, the New Place of the Tree of Life."

"I suppose it is worth mentioning that the Venus pentacles and stripes, or stars and stripes to be diplomatic, used to create the flag for the United States, came from the Barnsdale Washington's coat of arms. If you visit the Washington tombs in Barnsdale you will see the design in stone. There is also a colourful explanation of this particular inspiration for the design of the flag inside Selby Abbey, just up from Barnsdale."

"So, the Holy Grail, how does it fit into everything? You said the Grail was not the Grail or something."

"The Grail is just one of the names used to describe something that we need to complete the quest, immortality."

"Immortality, the Tree of Life?"

"Exactly. The Grail is the Tree of Life."

"Can you prove this?

"Of course."

The Grail and the Tree of Life

Again, I was instructed to drive, but this time Lily was wide awake and she laid out for me the entire history of King Arthur and the Holy Grail, beginning with King Arthur himself.

"Very little is known about King Arthur. In fact the first we hear of him is in the *Annals of Wales*, which, in effect, were written many centuries after his death. According to these annals, it was at the Battle of Badon that Arthur carried on his shoulders the True Cross, the cross of Jesus Christ, for three days and nights until the Britons were victorious."[4]

"So the cross that Jesus was crucified on came here too?"

"Indeed. And this is what we are heading towards, back in Barnsdale."

"The True Cross is in Barnsdale?"

"It was between 1180 and 1220 when the surge of literature concerning King Arthur, his round table and the Grail appeared. But these stories are thought to be based on several lost originals. From 1180 elegant court stories, rhymes and romances began to shape the face of the Arthurian legend. And by the end of this literary cycle we were left with an intricate, tangled web of Grail stories, which seem to be of a Christian bias, but at the same time do not exclude the influence of Arabic and Jewish traditions."

"I suppose that's not surprising. They were all created at the time of the Crusades."

"The first meaty encounter between King Arthur's Knights and the Grail is in a poem written by Chretien de Troyes.[5] Here the Grail cannot be seen, as it is too bright, described as 'light blinding'. Probably the most important aspect of this story, which everyone seems to have missed, is that the perilous Grail knight, Percival, is given a sword of unknown origin. Here Percival is told that, if the sword was broken, he could restore it at the lake, near where its maker lived."

"Excalibur?"

"No. From this early beginning there are various continuations of the story, written by Gautier de Danans, Menassier and Gerbert de Monteielle.[6] In Gautier's first continuation, we pick up the story with another Grail knight, Gawain, who is declared unfit to achieve the 'mysteries of the Grail'. But as part of the story, Gawain is presented with the same mysterious sword, this time broken, and he is told to go and mend it. But, unlike Percival, he does not know the location of the sword's maker and so he fails the task."

"OK."

"The writer, Gautier, then returns to Percival, on his quest to find the Grail castle. Here Percival is told that the Grail was given to people of the earth at the time when Jesus died on the cross. As part of the Grail mystery, Percival is also shown something."

"What?"

"At tree of pure light and a chapel from which its bright light shines."

"A shining tree and a chapel. Got you."

"Eventually Percival stumbles onto a castle that he has been seeking, where he knows he will be able to ask questions pertaining to the true nature of the Grail. But before Percival is given the answers to his questions, he is told to mend the sword. At this point Gautier ends his story, but it is picked-up by the Jewish writer Menassier, around 1220. Here we are told that Joseph of Arimathea had taken certain artefacts from the crucifixion to Britain."

"What artefacts?"

"Now, in the third continuation of the story, written by Gerbert de Monteielle, we hear about Percival's visit to the sword maker at the lake. Here we are told that the special sword had been forged a long time ago, and had been used at the gates of the Garden of Eden to guard the way to the Tree of Life."

"What, the same flaming sword used by the griffins in both the *Genesis* and the Gnostic creation stories?"

"Unfortunately we are never told who broke the sword. But my guess is that, metaphorically, it would have to be one of the adepts that will eventually pass through the gateway and take part in the final battle."

"So these Grail stories hold a message for the future adepts, those who might complete the quest?"

"But there is of course only one sighting of the Grail in all the romances, which explains just what it is."

"What, a cup?"

"This particular romance, *Parzival*,[7] one of the earliest written, was put together by a German crusader Knight called Wolfram Von Eschenbach. In this encounter, the scene is set inside the Grail Castle, and there is a procession, which includes the Grail Queen, who is holding the Grail itself."

"So what is it?"

"The description has eluded scholars. But if they knew what we know, then it would be blatantly obvious to them."

"Come on, spill the beans."

"Before I read out the description, I must explain that an 'Achmardi' is basically an ornate cloth."

"OK."

"Upon a deep green Achmardi she bore the pride of Paradise, root and branch beyond all price, that was a thing men call the Grail."

I thought about it for a moment, playing back all the evidence she had put before me.

"It is indeed obvious. The Grail can only be one thing. It will give us immortality as part of the quest to regain Paradise. It is the pride of Paradise, both root and branch, the Tree of Life."

"Bingo. Is that your final answer?"

"Well, what else could it be?"

The True Cross and the Tree of Life

As we approached the slip road for Robin Hood's Well, Lily pointed forward and asked me to keep driving.

"Just a little further and turn right into Barnsdale. We are heading for St. Helen's Church, next to the convent."

"I know it well."

After navigating down a familiar winding road, I turned into the rugged stretch that led down to St. Helen's. We got out, circled the church and then headed inside. The church was empty, apart from the vicar who was going about his business. He turned to us as we entered into the church.

"Can I help you?"

"Is it alright just to sit?" asked Lily.

"Of course."

The vicar exited through a small wooden door and Lily began.

"St Helena or St. Helen, in the British Tradition, was the daughter of the 4th century King, Coel of Colchester. You will probably know him as Old King Coel."

"What, the merry old soul?"

"Very good. In 1129, a man named Henry of Huntingdon wrote that the Holy Roman Emperor, Constantious, after conquests in Gaul and Spain, came to Britain.[8] While here, Constantious had a certain disagreement with King Coel, but due to the ingenious actions of Princess Helen, Coel's daughter, later St. Helena, the dispute was resolved, and Helena ended up marrying the Roman Emperor. From this union the most famous of all Roman Emperors was born, Constantine."

"Constantine from outside the Minster?"

"As you know, in the year 306 Constantine was proclaimed Holy Roman Emperor at Eborakon, present day York. In fact, I suggest you visit his statue again, and be sure to look at the sword that he is proudly exhibiting."

"Don't tell me it's broken?"

"In 1125, William of Malmesbury wrote that Constantine was born in Britain.[9] And a little later, Geoffrey of Monmouth added to Henry of Huntingdon's genealogy, stating that King Arthur was a descendant of Constantine.[10] Now, just after Constantine's death in 337, Eusebius documented the extent of what is known as the Vision of Constantine,[11] his vision of the True Cross. Apparently, before his death, Constantine confirmed by oath that he saw in the sky, above the setting sun, a luminous cross inscribed with the words, Εν Τοντω Νικα, which in Latin is, *In Hoc Signo Vinces*, and in English means, 'In this sign you shall conquer'. The sign of the True Cross."

"In this sign, not with this sign?"

"If you ever choose to visit the Apostolic Palace at the Vatican, you will see a painting of Constantine's Vision of the Cross. It was produced by the assistants of Raphael."

"A trip to Rome. Would you like me to book the flights?"

"Stop flirting. The idea of *In Hoc Signo Vinces*, 'In this sign you shall conquer', was explained to Constantine in a dream. In short, Jesus told him that if he used the symbol of the True Cross in battle, he would be victorious. Later, this Christianised battle standard was termed the 'Blood Red Cross'."

"Jesus' blood on the cross. I see."

"The image of the Blood Red Cross was sacred to early Roman Christians, ultimately used for the Arms of the Christian slayer of the Pagan dragon, St. George. As an Englishman, you will be well-aware of its significance. Moreover, you live in York, and you will have noticed that the Red Cross has been adopted by the city."

"So the Red Cross is symbolic of the True Cross, the one Jesus was crucified on?"

"According to these stories and legends, while in her seventies, Constantine's mother, St. Helena, set upon a journey to the Holy Land; and many things have been written about her achievements there. For example, she found the so-called Spear of Destiny, the nails from the

True Cross, the cup of the Last Supper and many more things. I believe, as part of his master plan, Hitler was hell bent on acquiring these relics.[12] Thank God he did not acquire them."

"What, Hitler was involved in all this?"

"The balance between good and evil, both on earth and above, is, as you know, an integral part of the quest. Hitler demolished the occult fraternities in Germany, looking for clues about the quest. Of course, when he outlawed Freemasonry, he aimed to take possession of their secrets.[13] But, as we know, the secrets have been lost to the Freemasons, just the symbolism remains. And even after the torture of the highest Masons, Hitler gleaned very little. But let's not talk about this dark side."

"Yes. It's not something that..."

"So, St. Helena was in fact most commonly associated with unearthing the Blood Red Cross, the True Cross itself, the Lignum Crucis, the same cross that Constantine had dreamt about, the cross of the crucifixion."[14]

"This church is named after St. Helena. I hope you are not going to suggest..."

"As explained in the legends, St. Helena found the site where the True Cross had been buried after the crucifixion, and to prove its authenticity she placed a corpse upon it, which in turn came back to life. The obvious intention of such stories was to give special power to this ultimate Christian relic."

"A clever move I suppose."

"St. Ambrose, the Bishop of Milan, first preached about Helena's discoveries in the year 395; and by the beginning of the 5th century a composite legend of St. Helena's discovery of the True Cross was circulating around Christendom."

"So what's your point?"

"Well, in a modern book the authors, Thiede and D'Ancona, go to great lengths to document the holistic implications of the story of St. Helena and the True Cross.[15] What interests me most about their book is the information regarding the origin of the wood that was used to manufacture the True Cross."

"Origin?"

"Yes, the origin of the wood. They explain that, to this day, the skull of Golgotha is representative of the skull of Adam, the skull from which the Tree of Life first took root, here, on earth. The same tree that was used to manufacture the True Cross."

"Golgotha, Adam's skull, the Tree of Life, the True Cross. I see where you are going with this. Very clever."

"This particular comment by the authors was undoubtedly inspired by something called the *Golden Legend*,[16] which was compiled around 1260. It contains various stories regarding the Christian Saints and their relics, but most importantly, the legend concerning the True Cross."

"Which was made from the Tree of Life."

"When Adam died, an Archangel gave a seed from the Tree of Life to Seth, his third son. Seth then placed the seed in his father's mouth, and from this both root and branch grew to form the Tree of Life on earth."

"I have not heard this story, but the concept somehow feels familiar, as if I have seen a depiction of the Tree of Life growing from Adam's mouth or something."

Lily laughed.

"I assume you visited many Minsters and Cathedrals when looking into the quest."

"Yes, York of course, Southwell, Ripon, Beverley, but to name a few."

Lily opened her lap top and quickly found what she was looking for (fig. 88).

Figure 88

"Does he look familiar?"

"Of course, the Green Man."

"The Green Man, Adam, with the Tree of Life sprouting from his mouth."

"That's fantastic. No one has ever been able to work out who the Green Man was. He appears in most Gothic Minsters and Cathedrals. Another ancient mystery solved then. So where was Adam buried?"

"At Golgotha."

"Is there any significance to the place name?"

"*Golgotha* means, 'The Place of the Skull', Adam's skull. According to the legend, around BC 1000, the wood from the Tree of Life was used to fashion a bridge, which was later crossed by the Ethiopian Queen, the Queen of Sheba, on a visit to see our old friend, King Solomon. On crossing the bridge she had a premonition about the future use of the wood, which she explained to Solomon would play a part in the future reformation of his faith. Fearing the worst, Solomon decided to dismantle the bridge and buried it."

"Where?"

"Back at Golgotha. The legend then goes on to say that the wood was later dug-up and used to make the cross of the crucifixion."

"So Jesus was crucified on a cross made from the Tree of Life. He was crucified on the Grail. Is this why he came back to life?"

"Good observation."

"And Sheba's premonition about the wood; she must have seen it at the crucifixion, the basis for Christian belief. This is why Solomon feared it. It would help form a new faith that went against his."

"Again, good observation."

"What about the skull on religious paintings that depict the crucifixion? It is always placed just under the cross. Is this representative of Adam's skull? Wait a minute, the Hans Holbein's painting, *The Ambassadors*, it has a skull in the picture, somehow disguised. Has this got something to do with it?"

"After the crucifixion, the wood was once again buried; and in the early 4th century, as I have already explained, St. Helena, the mother of Constantine, dug it back up."

"So what did she do with it?"

"What happened to the cross after St. Helena acquired it is open to speculation. Generally though, it is accepted that the cross was broken up and scattered far and wide. But certain sources explain that it was taken by Helena to a secret place, for safe keeping."

"Where?"

"As I have said, there are many theories regarding the fate of the True Cross, but for our purposes, if we are to follow a strand of the mystery that no one has followed before, we need to go back to the quote from the *Annals of Wales* again, which states that, around the 6th century, at the Battle of Badon, King Arthur, a descendant of Constantine and St. Helena, was in possession of the True Cross."

"King Arthur had the pride of Paradise, the Tree of Life. Of course, the Grail."

"You are enjoying this?"

"Immensely."

"It is chronicled that our old friend, Edward I, the one who placed Jacob's Pillar in the Chapter House, was also looking to acquire the True Cross, the Tree of Life, for obvious reasons."

"So did he find it?"

"In the *Chronicle of Lantercost*,[17] under the year 1282, it states that Edward I defeated the Welsh and took their treasures from the time of King Arthur. When I read what he found amongst their treasures, I realised the importance of my find."

"He found it, didn't he?"

"He found a most beautiful piece of the True Cross, carved into a portable cross, which was said to be the glory of their domain, which Helena had kept and brought with her when she returned to Britain."

"So what did Edward do with it?"

"Edward kept the Cross of Destiny or Cross Neyth and paraded it through the streets of London in May 1285. He also took the cross with him on journeys and campaigns, even when he removed Jacob's Pillar from the monastery at Scone."

"The two most important artefacts of the quest in one place."

"In March 2004, on the eve of Easter Sunday, I was sitting right here, and I was told a story about this church."

"Who by?"

"One of the congregation. They told me that the church had gained its name because of a visit by none other than St. Helena herself."

Lily stood up, walked across the stone floor and took hold of one of the leaflets that explained about the church's history.

"According to the story here, on one of her journeys to York, Helena stopped off at the Roman fort in Barnsdale,[18] which was situated just at the back of Robin Hood's Well. She then went off to pray at a local religious site, a Brigante site. And due to this gesture a small church was built to commemorate her visit. It has of course changed over the centuries, and at one time was owned by Robert de Lacy, but we are now at the site on which St. Helena came to pray."

"So you are intimating that the True Cross was actually brought here, to Barnsdale."

"It's a theory."

"So did the Grail, the Tree of Life, eventually make it into the temple, the Chapter House?"

"Of course. Oh, before I forget, I must read the little ditty that is written on the back of this leaflet."

Lily cleared her throat.

"Faith, yonder is the place and yonder the tree. I have seen the sun break through and illuminate a small field for a while and gone my way and forgotten about it, the one field that had the treasure in it."

15th Degree

Prophetic Processions

The long summer holiday had passed by in a flash. Only a week remained and I wanted to be with her, Lily, as much as possible. She had promised that she would get back in touch, but four days had gone by and no phone call or email. What was I to do? Fearing that I might never see her again I switched on my computer and began looking for something that might provide the final pieces to this global, esoteric jigsaw. But I knew deep down that without Lily's help I would never find a resolution.

Interpretations

After a little research, I soon discovered that very little was written about King Edward's involvement with the esoteric practices of the time. But I did know that he had a great interest in relics, which purportedly had great power. His portfolio of relics was quite extensive. He had plundered many treasure houses, taking from the Welsh the crown of King Arthur and the True Cross, and from the Scottish the Stone of Destiny, Jacob's Pillar.

I realised that such actions by Edward were tinged with dynastic and political overtones, and this was exemplified at Edward's Round Table event at Nefyn, in Wales, where he promised that he would provide the Welsh with a Prince of Wales. But most intriguingly, in 1278, Edward re-interred the excavated bones of King Arthur at the high altar at Glastonbury, amidst great pomp and ceremony.[1] It was in this time that the Chapter House at York Minster was under construction.

I also discovered that Edward's uncle, Frederick II, King of Jerusalem and Emperor of the Holy Roman Empire, had founded the University of Naples, and his court at Palermo was a centre for learned men. Ironically, scholars believe that it was here that Wolfram von Eschenback wrote his Grail poem *Parzival*, in which the true nature of the Grail is revealed, the Tree of Life.

Frederick's vast knowledge and wide range of talents earned him the nickname *Stupor Mundi*, the 'Wonder of the World'. He was well-known for his involvement in magic, and he built a strange castle in southern Italy called Castel del Monte. When I looked into the historical accounts of this castle, which was built around thirty years before the Chapter House, I found that it had no moat and no drawbridge, and that it was most likely built to act as something other than a military fortress.[2] The castle was also constructed using a unique geometric, Ogdoad design, a sort of octagonal prism, which started alarm bells ringing.

As I dug deeper, I found that the castle had been the inspiration for Umberto Eco's esoteric work, *The Name of the Rose*. Having read the book many years ago, and with the Latin inscription about the rose from the Chapter House prominent in my mind, I started to realise that I was most likely onto something. Out of curiosity, I decided to type "Castel del Monte Grail" into a search engine, and was amazed to find reams of sites that talked about its association with the Grail.[3] If only Lily was here, I thought. She would know what it all meant.

I loaded up my email account, just in case she had tried to contact me, and there was a message. A sudden feeling of joy swept over me. "Mail me back and I will phone you," the message said. I hit the reply button, "I'm here." A few moments later the phone rang and I picked it up.

"Hello Lily."

"Hello back."

"I've just been looking into Castel del Monte, Edward and his mysterious uncle, Frederick II."

"The Wonder of the World."

"Yes indeed, the Wonder of the World."

"I told you to look in the stained glass, didn't I?

"Frederick's in the stained glass?"

"You know the window where you found the Masonic inscription, across from the Masonic chapel?"

"Yes, the one that the Masonic Grand Master did an engraving of."

"In the window you would have found the old arms for Jerusalem, the royal coats for Frederick II and Edward I; and many important elements of the quest, along with the Ogdoad Wheel of Fortune at the centre, all looked over by the Grand Master of the Knights Templar. It is basically paying homage to Edward, his lineage and his importance to the quest. He believed that he would be one of the ones to go."

"The ones to go?"

"One of the prophesised adepts that would pass through the gateway. Imagine what Edward had done to progress the quest. Crowned king at 33 years of age, he had a major hand in designing the Chapter House, the final temple, which he eventually used for his Parliamentary sittings in 1298. And he had been the one to bring together the sacred objects inside the temple, objects that would enable the quest to be completed."

"I suppose it makes sense."

"Edward also had the stained glass in the Chapter House embellished with his royal signature. He believed that his sacred, royal lineage, his divine right on earth, was linked to this greater purpose."

"So how does 2012 fit into all this then? How could Edward go at such an early date when the prophesy said otherwise?"

"As I have already explained, the prophesy can be interpreted in different ways. And yes, 2012 is important, since it signifies the beginning of the end. But it is certainly not the end, as you will eventually see."

"So he didn't pass through the gateway then?"

"I do believe the adepts that will prevail have never existed and do not now."

"So how can the quest be completed?"

"This is something you will have to work out for yourself."

"What, a riddle?"

"It's not a riddle."

"Oh, before I forget, you mentioned something about a French interpretation of the prophesy the other day. How does this fit in then?"

"For me, the most provocative series of events concerning the French interpretation arc back to the year 1070, when the Turkish Seljukian Sultans took Jerusalem from the more tolerant Islamic Arab Caliphate."

"That sounds like a mouthful."

"Under this new regime, the Sultans persecuted the Christians, defacing and destroying their most sacred places. But, unbeknown to just a select few, in the same year, 1070, members of an archaic order of Italian monks made their way from Calabria in Italy, arriving soon after at Orval, on the northern French border."[4]

"Monks from Orval?"

"Both the movement of the monks and the taking of Jerusalem by the Sultans were inspired by an event that was prophesised to take place in Jerusalem, in the year 1099."

"Event?"

"These Italian Monks, whose predecessors spanned back to the early Gnostics, were preparing for the final battle with the darkest of all forces."

"And who might that be?"

"The one in opposition to Paradise itself; the one who would be released from his prison after a thousand years had passed, the Devil."

"Now that's a beauty, the Devil."

"John wrote, in his *Revelation*, that Satan would be bound for a period of 1000 years, and on his release would head for Jerusalem to fight for the Messianic Throne. Now, since John had his vision in the year 99, after 1000 years we would find ourselves in the year..."

"1099."

"As we know, elements of the prophesy were not just contained in *Revelation*, and this is why this date was known to different branches of the quest's guardians. Even though it should have been a joint effort, inevitably, greed, power and misguided faith took over."

"So the Sultans had taken Jerusalem at this time because they were guardians of the quest? They were preparing for this satanic battle?"

"Just like the Gnostic monks, they were positioning themselves for a battle like no other before, in the holy City of Jerusalem."

"A battle with the Devil himself. What a mind blower."

"A battle that could result in an end to the quest; to the end of the prophesy."

"So who won?"

"The Gnostic monks believed that to stay true to this interpretation of the prophesy, the one to fight the good fight would be descended from King David, the Davidic line, the same line that scripture foretold the Messiah would come from."[5]

"So the monks were after a descendant of King David, Solomon's father?"

"On their arrival at Orval, in 1070, the monks obtained the patronage of a lady called Matilda of Tuscany, the Duchess of Lorraine, La Gran Contessa, later Queen of Italy. The monks were given land at Orval, and Matilda funded them to lay the foundations of a modest monastery. Now, Matilda was grandmother, some say aunt, to a very special man named Godfrey de Bouillon whose lineage can be traced through King Dagobert I, the Merovingian king, back through to the Desposyni and ultimately to Solomon and King David."

"Desposyni?"

"Desposyni was the term coined by Sextus Julius Africanus, a writer of the early 3rd century, to refer to the relatives of Jesus."

"So the monks had come all this way for Godfrey de Bouillon?"

"In 1079, at the age of 13, the monks began to prepare Godfrey for his destiny. At 19 years of age, in 1085, he began his real training, using the Christian cross-shaped sword in battle against the crescent moon-shaped sword of the Muslims, in the sacking of the Muslim learning centre of Toledo in Spain."

"The crescent and the cross."

"The monks had calculated that it would take no longer than four years to reach Jerusalem, and with this in mind a plan was put in place to fuel a reaction from the Vatican. With perfect timing, in 1095, a council was called at Clermont-Ferrand in France, where Pope Urban II gave a speech that whipped up religious zeal in both clergy and knight. In 1096 these enthused 'crusaders' put on their garments, which had been inspired by the vision of Constantine, a white tunic divided into quarters by a red cross, and set upon their journey to take Jerusalem."

"Puppets to the quest."

"On July 15, 1099, exactly 1000 years after John's vision, Jerusalem fell to the Christian forces. In line with the prophesy, aged 33, just like Edward was when he became king, Godfrey de Bouillon was installed as *Advocatus sancti Sepulchri*, 'Defender of the most sacred sepulchre', in Jerusalem."

"But why not work together with the other guardians?"

"As I said, greed, power and misguided faith."

"And did the Devil arrive?"

"To the monks' disappointment, Godfrey did not buy in to their prophetic ideas and refused to take the title of King of Jerusalem."

"So what happened?"

"In a twist of fate, still at the age of 33, Godfrey was killed by his tutors. He was replaced by a more willing soul, Baudouin, his younger brother, who was crowned as the first Christian King of Jerusalem, Baudouin I."

"So what happened next?"

"After a year or so had come and gone, there was no evidence to suggest that there was to be a satanic rebellion."

"Should there have been one?"

"Who knows? Maybe enough had been done to divert the rebellion. Maybe their interpretation of the prophesy was incorrect. But in 1118, nearly two decades after the capture of Jerusalem, a contingent of knights were welcomed by the new King of Jerusalem, Baudouin II, the cousin of Baudouin I. This well-known story goes that these knights, led by Godfrey of St. Omer and Hugh de Pagens, were given lodgings on the site where Solomon's Temple once stood."

"You mean the Knights Templar?"

"Very few know what they were up to, but many say that their true mission was to search for items of intrinsic, religious value, hidden in the caverns situated under Solomon's Temple."

"There are caverns under the temple? What Enoch's Temple?"

"The route taken by these so-called Templars was re-excavated in 1867 by Lieutenant Warren of the Royal Engineers. The extent of the re-excavation was illustrated on-site, for the *London Illustrated News* in 1870."

"So what did it look like?"

"The excavation route descends vertically downwards through rock, before radiating out into a series of minor tunnels under the site. On this re-excavation, Lieutenant Warren found a spur, remnants of a lance, a small Templar cross and a large part of a Templar sword. I believe the Templar archivist for Scotland, Robert Brydon, who you mention in your work, has ensured the preservation of these objects."

"So what were the Templars really looking for under the temple?"

"In short, documents about the quest, more information about the prophesy."

"Did they find anything?"

"Yes. But not everything was recovered by the British guardians of the quest."

"Recovered?"

"Edward used the plans from under the temple to construct the Chapter House. And when he died in July of 1307 as Patron of the English Knights Templar, King Philip of France immediately seized the opportunity to capture both the Templars' money and secrets. But he, just like the other tyrants through the ages, failed to secure any information about the quest."

"Didn't Walt Disney do a film about all this?"

"Yes, *National Treasure*, starring Nicholas Cage and Sean Bean from Yorkshire."

"I remember now. It explains how the Templars' secrets and treasures were hidden in New York, New Eborakon, and how the Freemasons became embroiled in the mystery."

"Of course there is no mention of the quest. According to many writers, the Templars' most important secrets were taken to Rosslyn and Rennes le Château."

"I see why they might say this."

"Yes, the Gnostic Occitan, Languedoc or Septomania area, which surrounds Rennes le Château in southern France, was specifically chosen by the Knights Templar; and in 1885, a priest called Francois Berenger Sauniere unearthed some ancient documents, beneath Rennes le Château, the Grail church, discovering what many say were the Templars' secrets."

"What secrets?"

"Again this story is well told by many, and it is said that these secrets were so important that Sauniere used them to bribe the Vatican for money and favours."

"Must have been hot stuff then?"

"As I said the other day, I found only one thing when I went to Rennes le Château. I've just mailed it to you."

I checked my email and opened the attachment (fig. 89).

Figure 89

"I see it."

"It's a depiction of the 8th Station of the Cross, inside the Grail church, where the documents were found."

"8th Station?"

"I think there are about fourteen in total. They depict the final hours of Jesus, the so-called Passion, when he is carrying the True Cross."

"So what's the mystery with this 8th station then?"

"The Station depicts a woman from Jerusalem with a child. It is not the fact that some say it is Mary Magdalene with Jesus' child, but what the child is wearing here."

As I looked closely at the Station, I noticed that the child was wrapped in Scottish Tartan or Plaid.

"Rosslyn?"

"Perhaps. Can you meet with me in the Chapter House?"

"Yes, no problem, when?"

"Now."

I put on my coat and made my way down to the Minster. I walked the familiar walk across to the Chapter House, but everything seemed different now. As I passed through the entrance I saw her sat there, alone. My heart fluttered.

The Grand Prophesy

"Go back," Lily yelled out.

I stopped in my tracks.

"Go back and tell me what you see on the walls of the corridor."

I did as she asked and saw the procession of Green Men lining the corridor.

"Green Men," I shouted out. "Loads of them, all the way down the corridor."

"You can come in now. Look around, what do you see?"

"Poetically?"

"No. What was the Chapter House designed for, in a practical sense."

"You mean all the stone seats built around the edge?"

"Yes."

"I believe they were and still are used for powerful, religious men to sit round and discuss their business and make decisions."

"So why do you think that Edward held his Parliamentary sittings here?"

"Because he built it, and all the stuff relating to the quest?"

"It's just that I saw a program a few years ago, a Tony Robinson thing, a Time Team Special, *The Real Knights of the Round Table* it was called."

"Must have missed that one."

"He suggested that the Chapter House was a version of King Arthur's Round Table."

"I suppose that would make sense, considering Edward's interest in King Arthur. He reinterred Arthur's bones, held Round Table events in Wales and, if you are telling me the truth, brought the Grail, the Tree of Life here."

"Yes, it all seems to add up."

"So do you know where the Grail is, and which stone is Jacob's Pillar?"

"Well, we could tear down all the walls and dismantle all the wooden bosses and ceiling beams to find out. But I doubt we could defend ourselves in court."

"No, I suppose not."

We both laughed, and then Lily said something in a slightly different accent.

"I assume it has something to do with the Ogdoad."

"Sorry."

"I assume it has something to do with the Ogdoad."

"Oh my goodness, it's you, isn't it, Lily, it was written on your badge?"

"I was wondering if you would ever work it out."

"I knew I had heard that voice somewhere before. But you look different."

"It's amazing how a pair of glasses and a hat can change things."

"So you were the guide in here, the one who told me about the Ogdoad. I asked you about the Toothache Man."

"That's right."

"You knew what I was up to back then?"

"As I have said, I will tell you everything when the time is right."

"I just can't believe that was you."

"Under this temple is the remains of a Druid henge that was built in eight parts, each symbolising the essence of life, death and rebirth, the Druid seasons."

"Druid seasons?"

Lily flipped open her laptop and turned it towards me (fig. 90).

"As you can see, the henge denotes the eight druid seasons; Ostara, beginning March 21st, on the Vernal

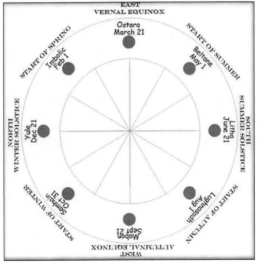

Figure 90

Equinox, the mid-point between the Druid spring and summer."

"Yes, the sun rises directly east on the Vernal Equinox."

"Then Beltane, the beginning of summer..."

"Look, Yule, Yuletide, Yuletide log, December 21st, Christmas time."

Lily laughed.

"You are surprised that Druid beliefs still play a part in modern culture?"

"Never really thought about it."

"If you look to the octagonal ceiling above, basically a Sun Wheel, found in most cultures, you will notice the eight, large, circular bosses that depict the eight seasons."

"Yes I see them."

"This denotes the Sun Wheel, a solar year of around 365 days. Of course, all the original artwork on the Chapter House ceiling was painted over as it began to decay, but there is a record of what was contained in each of the eight ceiling compartments. I found a description of them in a work by Charles McCarter, in the *Friends of York Annual Report*."

"There were paintings on the ceiling? Of what?"

"The Procession of the Ages."

"No, sorry, you have me there."

"At the moment, if you look east on the Vernal Equinox, just before the sun rises, you will be looking, in an astrological sense, at the stars that make up the sign of Pisces. But because of something called the axial procession, the view of the stars on each Vernal Equinox is slightly different. If you were looking east just before Jesus was born, you would have been looking at Aries. Each year we are slowly moving around the zodiac."

"How fast?"

"Well, it is all based around the angelic essence 72. Basically, every 72 years the view changes by 1 degree. Just as Jesus was born we were moving into Pieces. This was part of the prophesy, which was also known to the Magi, the three wise men from lands afar."

"So that's how they knew to go to Jerusalem, they used this procession. So how does Jesus fit into all this then?"

"The answer to your question would require a book in its own right, but it basically resides with John the Baptist, the intended Messiah. You might want to look up the Alpha to Omega riddle on a statue featuring John the Baptist and Jesus at Rennes le Château. But it is of little relevance to us. Anyway, apart from the cross, what do Christians use to denote Jesus? You may have seen it stuck on the backs of cars."

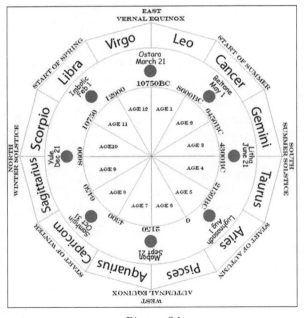

Figure 91

"Oh, you mean the fish."

"Yes the sign of Pieces, the Piscean Age. I have a full version of the procession here."

She turned the screen again (Figure 91).

"So, the Piscean age brought in by Jesus, as part of the prophesy, is due to come to an end soon, in relation to this massive cycle, and we will be moving into the Age of Aquarius. The dawning of the Age of Aquarius. Isn't there a song about this?"

"According to the prophesy in John the Divine's work, *Revelation*, the cycle began at the dawning of the Age of Leo, the first age."

I pointed to the screen.

"What, in BC 10,750?"

"Yes, in *Revelation* 4: 6-11, John states that the first beast was a lion, the second a calf, the third a man and the fourth an eagle."

"The Cherubin."

"Yes, the Lion as Leo, and if you draw a straight line across the procession, from the beginning to the end, where does it take you?"

Lily put up another image on screen (fig. 92)

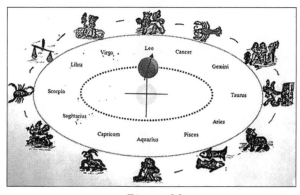

Figure 92

I moved my finger in a straight line, from Leo to its opposite sign on the zodiac, or procession.

"Aquarius, the sign of mankind, the Cherubin man."

"Yes, just like the Sphinx next to the Great Pyramid, with the body of a lion and face of a human, which was constructed to symbolise the first and last age."[6]

"The Lion and Human, the line across the procession, beginning and end."

"Now complete the grand cross. Cross the procession."

I placed my finger on Taurus and drew a line to Scorpio, making a perfect cross.

"So we have the lion, Leo, the calf, Taurus and the human, the sign of mankind, Aquarius. But what about Scorpio, the scorpion, it does not correspond to the eagle, like the Cherubin?"

"No it does not, but what you have to understand is that Scorpio is the most complex sign of the zodiac, embracing life, death and resurrection. And the sign has three corresponding symbols; the scorpion, phoenix and the eagle."[7]

She put another image on screen (fig. 93)

"So it all fits then. But what does it mean?"

Figure 93

"Think about where we are sitting in the Chapter House, east. What do you think was painted above us in the ceiling when the Chapter house was first constructed?"

"A human?"

"No, a lion."

"To represent the first age."

"And if we sat here in the east and turned the ceiling around, as if to turn around the ages, until Aquarius was sitting in the east, just before the rising sun; what do you think would be painted above us."

"A human?"

"No, wrong again, the Cherubim from *Revelation*, the face of a lion, bull, human and an eagle, the summation, the beginning and end, alpha to omega."

"When the quest will be completed; *Revelation*, the disclosure of secrets to man, by the divine."

"In 1924, a structural engineer and Egyptologist called David Davidson from Leeds, Yorkshire, published a monumental work on the Egyptian version of the temple, the Great Pyramid, which he entitled, *The Great Pyramid: Its Divine Message*.[8] Davidson discovered that the pyramid, just like the Chapter House, was built to act as an astronomical calendar. In this case, the very geometry of both its internal and external structures depict an astronomical chronology. Interestingly, he discovered that this chronology had an end time."

"What, the year 2150, the dawning of the Age of Aquarius?"

"Not quite, 2045"

"That's just over a hundred years out."

"Yes, but you have to understand that the dawning of any new age cannot be calculated perfectly. A variation of 100 years in the Procession of the Ages is neither here nor there."

"So, basically, the great pyramid is also defining the end time?"

"Undoubtedly. You state in your own work that it was one of the temples built to access the celestial realm."

"So I do."

She was but inches away from my face, her curled lips slightly raised, and she was staring into my eyes. I couldn't help myself. I just had to kiss her. To my surprise she kissed me back.

She suddenly pulled away.

"Are you satisfied now?"

I fell away and put my head down like a scolded child.

"Are you satisfied with the explanation of the procession?"

"Yes. Yes, it is more than I could have ever imagined."

16th Degree

The End Time

This time Lily and I had made arrangements to meet again in the Chapter House, on the Friday evening. I knew that we would only be in there for a short while, since the Minster would be closing. But I said nothing at the time, or when I took up the stone seat next to her when I arrived at the Chapter House. Without a word she took hold of my hand and guided me to the door that led to the secret, Rosicrucian room.

Down the Rabbit Hole and Beyond

"It will be locked," I said.

"Not tonight."

She pulled the door ajar and we both slipped in.

"We can wait in here until the Minster closes."

We made our way up the spiral staircase and sat on a ledge next to the floor containing the Master Stonemason's geometric tracings of the Chapter House's mystical compartments. She took out her laptop, opened it up and turned it towards me (fig. 94).

"This image comes from a work written by one of Bacon's fellow adepts, Henry Peacham. Peacham produced his work *Minerva Britanna* in 1612,[1] which

Figure 94

contains a collection of Rosicrucian emblems, holding various hidden meanings. On the title page of his book is this emblem that signifies the Rosicrucian quest; to draw aside the veil, to reveal the hidden secret."

"Yes, I see the ending, Ebor, Eborakon."

"If you draw aside the veil, by the mind it shall be seen. *Mente videbor*, 'by the mind I shall be seen."

Lily loaded up another image (fig. 95).

Figure 95

"Do you recognise this photograph? You received it around 2000. You contacted the British Museum to find out its origin."

As soon as I saw the picture it all came flooding back. When I had moved to York, just before I began my journey to follow the White Rabbit, I had purchased a house that had previously been rented by someone that was in touch with their 'spiritual side'. For many months following the move, I had the pleasure of receiving junk literature based around the ancient art of astrology. Aside from the articles that held promises of lottery wins and new found love when I saw the letter 'L', I received an offer to purchase a set of miniature magic pyramids, aptly named, "The 7 Pyramids of Kheops".[2]

As part of the booklet associated with the offer, there was an "official report" by a certain "International Commission of Enquiry" that deemed Mr Sophros, the creator of the 7 Pyramids, a great threat to public safety. It urged all governments to ban the circulation of his secret of the 7 pyramids, since in the wrong hands it could be detrimental to the human race itself. At the time, as I laughed and continued to flick through the booklet associated with the offer, I noticed that they had used several original photographs that had been taken in and around the Great Pyramid of Egypt in times-gone-by. And the photograph that Lily had on screen was the very one that caught my eye. It was a photograph of the inside of the King's Chamber with my surname, "Hewitt", inscribed at the back of the Pharaoh's or King's Coffer. That is, the coffer which he was placed in before he began his journey to the celestial realm.

At the time, out of curiosity, I decided to see if the person who had inscribed the name at the back of the coffer was a relation. So I contacted the British Museum, and John Taylor, Assistant Keeper of the Department of Ancient Egypt and Sudan, gave me the contact details of someone that might be able to help, Dr Lisa French, who I eventually emailed:

Hello Lisa,

John Taylor pointed me in your direction. I have added an attachment which I hope you can help me with. It is from the King's Chamber in the Great Pyramid. The image intrigued me, since the surname on the wall at the back of the King's Coffer is mine. It appears to say "W G HEWITT". Could you help me with the date of the photograph and/or the identity of the person that put the name there?

Thanks,

Richard Hewitt.

The next day I received a reply:

I am forwarding your message and picture to one of our members who deals with graffiti on the Giza site. I expect he will get back to you direct.

Lisa French, ASSTENE

A few days later I got a response from the graffiti expert:

Dear Sir, R. Hewitt,

Here with some information, in answer from a letter of Dr L. French, unfortunately I found not the right W.G.Hewitt only a G.Hewitt and B.Hewitt, both with no date and outside near top of pyramid. Sorry.

Kind regards,

Roger O. De Keersmaecker.

Belgium.

I turned to Lily.

"How did you get hold of this?"

"Did you know your paternal grandfather?"

"No, he died when I was very young."

"And when was he born?"

"I know that one. He was born on July 31, also my birthday. We were both born on the same date. I always found that a little weird."

"And so I assume you know nothing about his lineage, your lineage?"

"No, nothing. What are you trying to tell me?"

"I think you know."

"So you are saying that several of my relatives visited the Great Pyramid, and that one of them carved their name at the back of the King's Coffer? What for? A message?"

"Would you like a drink? We could be here for a while."

Lily again took out her flask and poured out what smelt like herbal tea. She took a small drink and passed it to me. I took a slurp.

"That tastes really, well, different."

"It's my own blend. Drink up, it's good for you."

"So where does all this end Lily?"

She said nothing for a long while and then suddenly proposed something that sent a shiver down my spine.

"It all ends here, tonight."

Unable to help it, I belched and a stream of acid entered my mouth. I swallowed.

"Sorry, your tea seems to have disagreed with me. Why tonight? How tonight?"

"You will see."

"By the way, I looked up your name, Lilith. Do you know what it means?"

"Yes, I do as a matter of fact. It is the name of a character from the Babylonian Talmud, the head of the female demons."

"Really. What I found is that, in Jewish folklore, Lilith was the first wife of Adam, basically the same as Eve of Life in the Gnostic creation story; the one who educated Adam and told him about the true nature and intentions of the Authorities."

"Yes, I know of that interpretation too. Have you ever heard of Zipf's Law?"

"Zip what?"

"I was talking to a professor the other day and he said that he was working on a theory about how to access a message that is written into our DNA, specifically our junk DNA. Did you know that it makes up 97% of us?"

"What does?"

"Junk DNA."

A larger surge of acid bellowed up into my mouth.

"Your tea is definitely doing strange things to me. So you are saying that only 3% of our DNA is of any use to us?"

"Well, I suppose that is one way of looking at it. Zipf's Law, it's quite a strange law, but basically it can be used to prove that all languages around the world have a common structure, and what scientists have discovered is that junk DNA has the same structure, it's basically a language, it is a story, words, a message from the beginning."[3]

As I focused in on Lily, I started to see strange shards of light, almost like miniature streaks of lightening.

"That's really weird."

"The professor said that he was looking into the idea that certain tribes, for many years, have inadvertently been gaining access to this DNA language, to this message, when taking part in spiritual ceremonies, rituals, using various natural enhancers. You know hallucinogens."

"Using drugs to see into our very construct. That's a fascinating idea."

"It does make you think though. What if there is a message written into our DNA? If we could access it, would it reveal the true nature of the Philosophers' Stone, the blueprint of the temple, the entire nature of our purpose in life, the quest?"

"You mean just like the message that is rendered into the architecture of this temple, the Chapter House's architecture, there could be a message inside us from the Grand Architect himself."

Suddenly I felt very queasy. I began to wretch.

Lily stood up and walked towards the staircase.

"Not long now."

In an instance it dawned on me what Lily had done. She had given me more than just herbal tea. Another burst of acid solution entered my mouth.

"You have to be kidding me. What have you given me?"

"Don't worry it's not what you think. Just let it happen."

"Happen?"

"Don't fight it. It will make no difference anyway."

I tried to stand up, but started to tremble and soon after lost my balance. I started laughing uncontrollably. Sweat was now dripping down my forehead. The discomfort in my stomach was building. Everything was beginning to spin. I closed my eyes for a second, maybe a minute. I seemed to lose all sense of time. It all went black.

It came slowly, but then speeded up. I was nowhere yet moving towards something. Out of a dull, twirling kaleidoscope of colours a vivid network of roots suddenly appeared, just like the one in my dream with the White Rabbit; roots that shone like stars.

"What have you done to me?"

I knew I was saying the words, but could not hear them. I came round for a second and then the shining roots reappeared. A sudden feeling of weightlessness took over. I was being raised up through the roots, to the surface. I was now above the ground, passing by a silky tree trunk that was supporting branches with golden leaves and fruits that looked like edible rubies, sparkling, filled with some sort of green nectar that was dripping into the purple grass.

"What have you given me?"

Somewhere in the distance I heard a sweet voice.

"Eboka, dogbane. Don't worry, I know the correct dosage."

I suddenly came back round, but it didn't last long. Lily had wrapped my arm around her neck and she was guiding me down the swirling, stone staircase.

"It has always been done this way. Shamans have used it from the beginning to resurrect their Third Eye."

"Third Eye," I slurred.

I was now lying at the centre of the Chapter House. Lily was there, but she was not. And I could feel someone or perhaps something else. She had drugged me, given me some sort of hallucinogenic potion.

"Open your mind's eye," a voice whispered and it all went white.

In a blink of an eye everything suddenly shifted. I was being transported, flung down a seemingly endless, glimmering warren, a rabbit hole, then a worm hole, left and right, up and down. And then out into the blackness, weightless, as if I had been on a galactic slide that had catapulted me into the darkest recesses of the universe.

I slowly drifted down, and there I was, standing yet not standing at the centre of the temple. It all seemed calm now, and I was facing east, watching the rising sun. They were all watching me, the anonymous stone faces that had somehow come to life, chanting sounds that suddenly turned into a strange language that I sort of understood. As I listened closely, the sounds became a feeling, then a vision. I could see a silver ladder, but then it disappeared, a tree of pure light and then it all turned grey. I screamed as a weird, demonic head swiftly circled round the chapter house and made a last turn, stopping inches from my face, opening its mouth until it extended over its bristly head, revealing its rusty, razor sharp teeth. I screamed again as the head exploded and left a red, watery mist that faded into nothing. I was strangely calm again, and a whisper sounded out.

"They reside in you," it uttered from the abyss. "They reside in you."

I called out.

"They reside in me?"

"You are from the beginning."

"Beginning?"

"In the beginning was the Word, and the Word was with God, and the Word was God."

I could see a question floating down from the pinnacle of the temple. I opened my mouth and it entered.

"And the end?"

"Alpha to omega. To those who overcome I will give to eat of the Tree of Life. Say unto me I am that I am, hidden in the light, in the Rose of Sharon, I will be that

I will be. The age is upon us. 2012 is just the beginning. Revisit us in this time."

And then there was nothing.

Revelation

I could feel the sun on my cheek, not too strong, as if it were somehow masked. I swallowed and the taste of acid reignited in my mouth. I felt a warm mass against my back and a cotton substance clenched in my hand.

The sweat from my forehead had formed a crust between my eyelids and it stung slightly as I opened them. I was in my own bed. I turned over and was facing the sleeping beauty, the one that had given me the poisonous brew. After a few flickers her large brown eyes were gazing into mine.

"I'm sorry, but tell me, what did you see?"

"What did I see? What do I see? I see you, Lilith. You tricked me."

"No, I only wanted to know if you would see what I saw."

"Then why didn't you just ask?"

"Would you have done it?"

"No."

"I rest my case."

"But that doesn't give you..."

"Relax. Tell me what you saw."

"What I saw. I went on a journey and they told me that 'they reside in me'. Who resides in me? And that I should say unto them 'I am that I am, hidden in the light, in the Rose of Sharon, I will be that I will be.' What does it mean?"

"Similar words are written on a scroll."

"What scroll?"

"The one kept at Lodge Kirkwall, Kilwinning.[4] I will take you to see it one day."

"So what did you see Lily? Did they say the same to you?"

"The same. We have to return in 2012, and they reside in me also."

"Who?"

"Those who will eventually come to complete the final journey."

"The prophesised adepts?"

"Yes."

"Tell me everything."

She stretched down to the floor, picked up her laptop and held it to my face (fig. 96).

"I really don't know what will happen to us when we revisit the Chapter House in 2012, there is nothing written. But what I do know is that out of me, out of us will come the ones who will ultimately pass through the gateway to take part in the final battle and save it."

"Save what?"

"The final tarot, the only thing that matters."

"Speak English."

Figure 96

She paused for a long while, smiled and then whispered the fateful words that still haunt me to this very moment.

"*Le Monde*, 'The World'."

References and Notes

1st Degree

1. Of the many examples of the special relationship between Venus and the White Rabbit, two examples that help illustrate their astronomical connection can be found in Susan Milbrath, *Star Gods of the Maya*: *Astronomy in Art, Folklore, and Calendars*, p. 198 and Robert L. Hall, *An Archaeology of the Soul*: *North American Indian Belief and Ritual*, p. 87. It is also worth noting that in many ancient cultures both the White Rabbit and the goddess Venus were synonymous with rebirth, fertility and ultimately sexuality. This may explain why Hugh Hefner unwittingly chose the symbol for his magazine, *Playboy*.

2. In one Islamic tradition, an example of which can be found on the website http://iranpoliticsclub. net/islam/crescent-star/index.htm, it states that the Islamic crescent and star represent a conjunction of the Moon and Venus, which took place in the dawn sky of July 23, 610 AD, when the Prophet Mohammed received his initial revelation (Vahy) from Allah, via Angel Gabriel.

3. This Rosicrucian image (one of their so-called 'secret symbols') is referred to as both the *Philosophers Mountain* and the *Mountain of Initiation*. It appears in many secret society settings and is often attributed to the influential Rosicrucian-alchemist, Basilius Valentinus. The White Rabbit here is a metaphor for the illusive or possibly unattainable secret sought by the Rosicrucians. See Illustration Acknowledgements, 1st Degree Figures, 2 for a detailed account of the various sources for this image.

4. Contact details for the Paradise Lodge, 139 can be found at http://wrprovince.net/chapter-detail/?chapter=139

5. The idea that the White Rabbit in St. Mary's Church, Beverley, was the inspiration for Carroll's character is well established. For instance, references can be found to it on national travel websites, as illustrated at http://www.britainexpress.com/photo.htm?photo=2784

6. One good example of the pagan essence and subsequent destruction of misericords can be found at http://en.wikipedia.org/wiki/Misericord.

2nd Degree

1. Bacon's literary executor, Dr. Rawley, first published *New Atlantis* in 1627, the year after the author's death. The introduction is generally omitted from modern copies, appearing only in the

earliest versions. After research it seems that copy used by Thomas was published by Andrew Hebb, London, At the Bell in St. Paul's churchyard, c.1627.

2.   I later found details of the secret knowledge that had been rendered into the architecture of Solomon's temple, which is discussed in the 7*th* *Degree*. For reference purposes, it exists in Christianson, Gale E, *Isaac Newton*. Oxford University Press US, p. 144, 2005.

3.   See, for example, http://www.pantheon.org/areas/featured/solomon/ksqb-2.html

4.   Josephus, Flavius *Antiquities of the Jews*, translated by William Whiston, 1737, Book VIII, Chapter II, beginning Section 5.

5.   See, for example, S.L. MacGregor Mathers, *The Key Of Solomon*, from Add. MSS. 10862, 1889, Book 1, Part 1, British Library.

6.   After a little research I found that other versions of this particular magic circle appear in the Bodleian Library, Michael MS. 276. An equivalent also appears in a Latin version, Bodleian Library, Aubrey MS. 24, dated to 1674.

7.   A collection of the Gnostic texts from Nag Hammadi can be found at http://www.gnosis.org/naghamm/origin.html

8.   *On the Origins of the World*, Nag Hammadi Codex (II,5; XIII,2).

9.   For an academic version of the translation see, *On the Origins of the World*, Nag Hammadi Codex (II,5; XIII,2), as found in James M. Robinson, ed., *The Nag Hammadi Library*, revised edition, HarperCollins, San Francisco, 1990.

10.   See *The Testament of Solomon*, trans. F. C. Conybeare, *Jewish Quarterly Review* Vol.11, pp.15-45, October, 1898.

3rd Degree

1.   See, also, http://www.guardian.co.uk/world/2003/may/12/religion.schools.

2.   *The Testament of Solomon*, trans. F. C. Conybeare, *Jewish Quarterly Review* Vol.11, pp.15-45, October, 1898.

3.   For an academic version of the translation see, *On the Origins of the World*, Nag Hammadi Codex (II,5; XIII,2), as found in James M. Robinson, ed., *The Nag Hammadi Library*, revised edition. HarperCollins, San Francisco, 1990.

4.   Ibid.

5.   Ibid.

6.   Ibid.

7.   Ibid.

8.   Ibid.

9.   Ibid.

10. For example, see http://www.bible.gen.nz/amos/history/cherub.htm

11. For a more in-depth view of the role of the griffin and its association with protecting the Tree of Life and road to salvation, see http://www.monstropedia.org/index.php?title=Griffin

12. For example, see http://www.themystica.com/mystica/articles/n/numerology.html

13. http://en.wikipedia.org/wiki/216_(number)

4th Degree

1. See, R W. Rogers, *Cuneiform Parallels to the Old Testament* (New York, 1912).

2. Ibid, Part III, pp. 67-75.

3. Ibid

4. Ibid

5. Edwin Oliver James, *The Tree of Life: An Archeological Study*, Netherlands, 1966, p. 10

6. A good example of the cylinder seal depicting Tammuz and Gishzida can also be found in Zecharia Sitchin, *The 12th Planet*, Avon Books, 1978, p166.

7. See for example, *Le Triomphe Hermetique,* from *Collectanea chymica*, 1693 and *Le Triomphe Hermetique* Limojon de Saint-Didier 8°, Amsterdam, 1689.

8. An example of the cup can be found published as fig. 368c in William Hayes Ward, *The Seal cylinders of Western Asia*, Washington, 1910.

9. http://www.pantheon.org/articles/n/ningizzida.html

10. http://en.wikipedia.org/wiki/Thoth

11. http://www.ancientegyptonline.co.uk/thoth.html

12. http://www.newadvent.org/cathen/13193b.htm

13. *Mercurius Trismegistus*, found in Francofurti: Sumptibus Ludovicj Bourgeat, *Historia deorum fatidicorum*, 1680, plate opposite p. 37.

14. Bacon's literary executor, Dr. Rawley, first published *New Atlantis* in 1627, the year after the author's death. The introduction is generally omitted from modern copies, appearing only in the earliest versions. After research it seems that copy used by Thomas was published by Andrew Hebb, London, At the Bell in St. Paul's churchyard, c.1627.

15. http://en.wikipedia.org/wiki/Coptic_ankh

5th Degree

1. Having revisited the library to acquire the exact reference to the 16th century *Camdeni Britannia* volume, the librarian was unable to locate it. But a reference to the same pyramid forms can be found at http://www.philological.bham.ac.uk/cambrit/yorkslat.html

2. I later found evidence of this theory at http://www.
    bbc.co.uk/dna/h2g2/alabaster/A3136123 and
    http://www.crystalinks.com/thornborough.html

3. C. Knight & R. Lomas, *Uriel's Machine: The
    Prehistoric Technology That Survived The Flood*,
    Century, London, 1999.

4. See, for example, R H. Charles, *The Book Of
    Enoch*, Translated by R. H. Charles, London,
    1917.

5. Ibid, Chapter I.

6. Ibid, Chapter XXXIV.

7. Aturo de Hoyos, 33°, Article 1, The Mystery of the
    Royal Arch Word, Heredom, the Transactions of
    the SRRS, Volume 2, 1993.

8. Contact details for the original: http://www.
    worcestershirepgl.org.uk/cnm/index.aspx

9. George R. Riffert, *Great Pyramid Proof of God*,
    Stanhope Press, pp.66-67, 1932.

10. See for example: http://www.whitedragon.org.uk/
    articles/yew.htm

11. Ibid.

12. See http://www.thegoddesstree.com/trees/Yew.htm

13. See, for example: http://www.whitedragon.org.uk/
    articles/yew.htm

14. See Germanic Paganism and Norse Mythology:

http://en.wikipedia.org/wiki/Tree_of_life and
http://www.icon.co.za/~heinl/history.htm

15. See http://www.inthelight.co.nz/spirit/norsegods.
htm and http://ezinearticles.com/?The-Tree-of-Life-
and-Allies&id=38788

16. R H. Charles, *The Book Of Enoch*: Together with
a reprint of the Greek fragments, XXIV p. 52,
1917.

6th Degree

1. See http://en.wikipedia.org/wiki/Great_Architect_
of_the_Universe

2. Job 38:4

3. R H. Charles, *The Book Of Enoch*: Together with
a reprint of the Greek fragments, LXI, p. 119,
1917.

4. See http://www.ancientegyptonline.co.uk/
foundationritual.html#stretch

5. Information about the Nebra Sky Disk and the
appearance of the Pleiades cluster on its surface
can be found at http://www.bbc.co.uk/dna/h2g2/
A2207297 and http://en.wikipedia.org/wiki/
Nebra_sky_disk.

6. The same imagery can be found on a tracing board
from the 18th century at http://www.freemasons-
freemasonry.com/symbolism_tracing_boards.html

7. *First Degree*, International Co-Freemasonry (1925 Working Revised), p. 92.

8. An almost identical copy of this image can be found in the *First Degree*, International Co-Freemasonry (1925 Working Revised), pp. 88-89.

9. See Albert G. Mackey and H. L. Haywood *Encyclopaedia of Freemasonry*, Vol. 2, pp. 976-997, 1909.

10. Ibid, p. 976.

11. Albert G. Mackey, *The Symbolism of Freemasonry*, XXX, The Stone of Foundation, 1882.

12. See http://en.wikipedia.org/wiki/Philosopher's_stone

13. Ibid.

14. See, for example, http://www.world-mysteries.com/awr_alchemy.htm

15. See, for example, *Bulletin of the Atomic Scientists*, 40th Anniversary Issue, p. 39, August 1985.

16. Michael Maier, *Atalanta Fugiens, hoc est, Emblemata Nova de Secretis Naturae Chymica*, Oppenheim: Johann Theodori de Bry, 1617.

17. Ibid

1. See http://en.wikipedia.org/wiki/Milton_a_Poem

2. The legend regarding Jesus' visit to ancient Albion is a well establishes in what is called Glastonbury Lore. One interesting link which talks about a modern film that covers the legend is http://www.dailymail.co.uk/news/article-1230860/Was-Jesus-taught-Druids-Glastonbury-New-film-claims-possible-came-England.html

3. For the original etching, see, http://www.themorgan.org/collections/works/blake/work.asp?id=onDisplay&page=1

4. See http://www.themystica.com/mystica/articles/b/blake_william.html

5. See http://www.golden-dawn.com/eu/displaycontent.aspx?pageid=114-traditions-influencing-the-golden-dawn

6. See http://www.esotericgoldendawn.com/tradition_bio_westcott.htm

7. William Blake, JERUSALEM: The Emanation of the Giant Albion (1804).

8. Ibid.

9. An original version of this plate can be found at http://www.blakearchive.org/exist/blake/archive/object.xq?objectid=jerusalem.e.illbk.100&java=yes

10. Blake's drawing of Newton can be found at http://www.tate-images.com/results.asp?image=N05058&wwwflag=3&imagepos=1

11. See, *Newton and the Rosicrucians* at http://en.wikipedia.org/wiki/Isaac_Newton's_occult_studies,.

12. See, *Newton's studies of the Temple of Solomon.* http://en.wikipedia.org/wiki/Isaac_Newton's_occult_studies

13. Ibid. Quoted from Christianson, Gale E. (2005). *Isaac Newton.* Oxford University Press US. p. 144.

14. See, for example http://www.templemount.org/allah.html

15. See (2 Chr. 3:14; compare Exodus 26:33), as discussed in http://en.wikipedia.org/wiki/Solomon's_Temple.

16. 1 Kings 6:12.

8th Degree

1. See, for example, http://www.freemasonrytoday.com/51/p18.php?printnice=yes

2. See, for example, http://www.roman-britain.org/places/eburacum.htm and http://www.myetymology.com/proto-brythonic/Eborakon.html

3. See http://www.freemasons-freemasonry.com/prescott13.html

4. See, for example http://en.wikipedia.org/wiki/Godfrey_Higgins

5. See http://en.wikipedia.org/wiki/The_Druid_Order, (History section).

6. Details of this can also be found at http://www. freemasons-freemasonry.com/prescott06.html

7. Ibid.

8. Ibid.

9. Brian P. Copenhaver, *Hermetica: The Greek Corpus Hermeticum and the Latin Asclepius in a New English Translation with notes and introduction*, notes to page 6, I.26, region of the ogdoad, Cambridge University press, 1992, p. 117.

10. See Halfpenny. J, Gothic Ornaments in the Cathedral Church of York, Plate located to the back of the book, 1795. Proofs for the first addition can be found in York Local History Library.

9th Degree

1. See, for example, http://www.skyscript.co.uk/ venusrose.html and http://www.freemasons-freemasonry.com/pentagram_freemasonry.html

2. The image (centre) appears in, C. Larkin, *The Book of Revelation: A Study of the Last Prophetic Book of the Bible*, 1919, p. 89. The image (right) Private Collection is in the style of *Our Lady of Guadalupe* (Spanish: *Nuestra Señora de Guadalupe*), but it is most likely related to events in Revelation. The image (left) Private Collection.

3. Revelation 12: 1.

4. See http://eclipse.gsfc.nasa.gov/transit/venus0412.html

5. See, for example, http://2012-endofdays.com/ and http://en.wikipedia.org/wiki/2012_phenomenon

6. Revelation 2:7.

7. Revelation 3:12.

10th Degree

1. See, for example, http://www.craftmasonry.net/index.php?location=stonemasons/index

2. Many examples of this image exist, such as in a printed book issued in 1788, published by Joh. Ad. Eckhardt, Book-Printer to H.M. the King of Denmark, entitled, *The Teachings of the Rosicrucians of the 16th and 17th Centuries or A Simple ABC Booklet For Young Students Practising Daily in the School of the Holy Ghost Made clear to the eyes by pictorial figures For the Exercises of the New Year In the Natural and Theological Light by a Brother of the Fraternity of the Rose Cross Christi P.F. For the first time made public and with several figures of similar content added by P.S. Altona.* Also in the *Altona Manuscript*, published in 1785, under the title *Geheime Figuren der Rosenkreuzer*, or *Secret Symbols of the Rosicrucians*.

3. Vitruvius, Book III, Chapter 1, *The Planning of Temples*. The following link holds a translation of the work, http://www.vitruvius.be/boek3h1.htm

4. As seen on Robert Fludd's title page for *Utriusque cosmi historia*, Oppenheim, 1617.

5. Michael Maier, *Atalanta Fugiens, hoc est, Emblemata Nova de Secretis Naturae Chymica*, Oppenheim: Johann Theodori de Bry, 1617.

11th Degree

1. For information about the *Goetia* and links to the full text, see, http://en.wikipedia.org/wiki/Goetia

2. *The Testament of Solomon*, trans. F. C. Conybeare, *Jewish Quarterly Review* Vol.11, pp.15-45, October, 1898.

3. For more information about the appearance of the Shem Ha-Mephorash in these areas, see, Meegan, William J., "THE SISTINE CHAPEL: A Study in Celestial Cartography," *THE ROSE CROIX JOURNAL*, Volume 3, 2006 and http://en.wikipedia.org/wiki/Shemhamphorasch

4. A rendition of the Masonic degrees and associated tracing boards can be found in Charles T. McClenechan, *Book of the Ancient & Accepted Scottish Rite of Freemasonry*, 1884.

5. See, for example, http://www.rosicrucian-order.com/trad.htm

1. The feature can be viewed at http://www.
culturenorthernireland.org/article/2559/my-
cultural-life-paul-feldstein

2. This is an often used quote and can be found for
example at http://www.all-ireland.com/attractions/
people/yeats.htm

3. http://www.nli.ie/yeats/main.html

4. The notebook in question is referenced as NLI MS
36,277(2).

5. http://en.wikipedia.org/wiki/A._E._Waite

6. For an academic version of the translation see, *On
the Origins of the World*, Nag Hammadi Codex
(II,5; XIII,2), as found in James M. Robinson,
ed., *The Nag Hammadi Library*, revised edition.
HarperCollins, San Francisco, 1990.

7. See for example, http://www.meaningoftarot.
com/?page_id=47

8. The Antikythera mechanism was probably
constructed around BC 150, the first analogue
computer, based around astronomical calculations.
According to the following site, Michael Wright,
who has done extensive work on decoding the
mechanism, calculated that it had 72 gears: http://
en.wikipedia.org/wiki/Antikythera_mechanism

9. I did eventually look through the Pyramid Texts
and found the exact utterances using the following

site: http://www.sacred-texts.com/egy/pyt/index. htm. Utterances 21, 25, 45 and 215.

10. An example can be found at http://www.sacred-texts.com/tarot/tob/tob39.htm

11. See, http://en.wikipedia.org/wiki/Albert_Einstein_ in_popular_culture

12. As explained at http://www.buzzfeed.com/mjs538/ most-expensive-photo-of-albert-einstein-ever

13. See, http://wiki.answers.com/Q/Why_did_Albert_ Einstein_stick_his_tongue_out

13th Degree

1. For one good explanation of this see http://www. grahamphillips.net/books/hood.htm

2. Henry Care's association with Poor Robin's Intelligence can be found in, Lois G. Schwoerer, *The Ingenious Mr. Henry Care, Restoration Publicist*, The John Hopkins University Press, p.40, 2001.

3. There are many examples of this spelling, but one example can be found at http://www. schubertline.co.uk/Scorchshop/cgibin/showscore. pl?purcelltwaswithinb.sco&1314329890

4. For an in-depth study of this concept see, Alfred Dodd, *The Secret History of Francis Bacon*, The C. W. Daniel Company LTD, London, 1931. The idea is also covered at http://www.phoenixmasonry.

org/secret_teachings_of_all_ages/bacon_shakspere_
and_the_roscrucians.htm

5.   For a concise explanation of the well-established
       theory, see http://en.wikipedia.org/wiki/
       Barnsdale#Connections_between_the_Barnsdale_
       area_and_the_Robin_Hood_legend

6.   Anthony Munday, *The Downfall and The Death
       of Robert Earl of Huntington*, 1601.

7.   See, for example, http://midgleywebpages.com/
       honour.html

8.   *A Lyttell Geste of Robin Hode*. No one knows
       when the story was written, but it was most likely
       written by a mysterious religious writer, Bible
       translator, and hermit from Barnsdale called
       Richard Rolle (1290 – 1349)

9.   In *A Lyttell Geste of Robin Hode* the association
       is as follows: "I made a chapel in Barnsdale that
       seemly is to see, it is of Mary Magdalene, and
       thereto would I be." The words "it is of Mary
       Magdalene" means that it was an affiliate of a
       Mother House of that name, in this case, St. Mary
       Magdalene in Bretton. This is confirmed by the
       Bretton coat of arms, Archangel Michael holding a
       shield with three covered chalices, which can still
       be seen on the entrance to the chapel.

10.   Evidence of Robert de Lacy's involvement with
       the chapel can be found in the *Early Yorkshire
       Charters*, in the *Fee of Delacy*.

11. See Judith A. Frost, THE FOUNDATION OF NOSTELL PRIORY, 1109-53, Borthwick Paper 111; Borthwick Institute, University of York 2007

12. See, Dr. Gordon, *Ecclesiastic Chronicle for Scotland*, Vol. 3, p. 27, 1875 and http://en.wikipedia.org/wiki/Robert_of_Scone

13. Dr. Gordon, *Ecclesiastic Chronicle for Scotland*, Vol. 3, p. 30, 1875

14. For instance, see, Dr. Gordon, *Ecclesiastic Chronicle for Scotland*, Vol. 3, p. 27, 1875; The Scottichronicon (Chronicle of the Scottish Nation) John of Fordun, Chapter VIII – L, c. 1345; *The Book of the Taking of Ireland, Leabhar Gabhala.*

15. See, for example, http://creationwiki.org/Calcol and 1 Chronicles 2:6.

16. Andrew of Wyntoun's *Orygynale Chronicle* (c.1420).

17. For instance, see, Dr. Gordon, *Ecclesiastic Chronicle for Scotland*, Vol. 3, p. 27, 1875, The Scottichronicon (Chronicle of the Scottish Nation) John of Fordun, Chapter VIII – L, c. 1345 and *The Book of the Taking of Ireland, Leabhar Gabhala.*

18. John O'Donovan, *Annals, The Kingdom of Ireland by the Four Masters*, vol. 1, p. 31, Dublin, 1849.

19. Hector Boece, *The History and Chronicles of Scotland (Scotorum historiae a prima gentis origine)*, 1526.

20. See, http://ads.ahds.ac.uk/ catalogue/adsdata/ arch-352- 1/dissemination/pdf/arch_scot_ vol_004/04_366_369.pdf

21. John Evelyn, *Sylvia*, London, Henry Colburn, 1827.

14th Degree

1. For a detailed explanation of this theory, see, http://sinclair.quarterman.org/ca-ns.html

2. See, for example, Manly P. Hall, *THE SECRET TEACHINGS OF ALL AGES, Rosicrucian Doctrines and Tenets* p.141, 1928.

3. See, for example, http://www.adwick-st-laurence. co.uk/history_washington.html

4. The full quote from the *Annals of Wales* goes as follows: Year 72 (c. 519 AD), 'The Battle of Badon, in which Arthur carried the cross of our Lord Jesus Christ on his shoulders for three days and three nights and the Britons were victors'.

5. Chretien de Troyes, *Perceval, the Story of the Grail*.

6. A list of the continuations of the story can be found at, http://en.wikipedia.org/wiki/ Perceval,_the_Story_of_the_Grail#Manessier.27s_ Continuation

7. Wolfram Von Eschenbach, *Parzival*.

8. Henry of Huntingdon, *Historia Anglorum*, also known as, *Historia ecclesiastica gentis Anglorum*, first printed by Sir Henry Savile in 1596, but believed to have been put together in 731.

9. William of Malmesbury, *Gesta Regum Anglorum*, 1125.

10. Geoffrey of Monmouth (c. 1100 – c. 1155), *Historia Regum Britanniae*.

11. Eusebius of Caesarea, *Vita Constantini*, 337.

12. See, for example, Ravenscroft, Trevor, *The Spear of Destiny*, Samuel Weiser, Inc. 1982.

13. See, for example, http://freemasonry.bcy.ca/anti-masonry/hitler.html

14. According to Jerome, Gelasius of Caesarea's (d. 395) writings were never published, but in the fifth century Socrates Scholasticus cites some of his works, which suggest that he wrote a sequence to Eusebius' history, preserved in the first fifteen chapters of Rufinus' tenth book that added to Eusebius' history, which is probably the earliest mention of the legend of Helena's discovery of the True Cross.

15. Thiede & D'Ancona, *The Quest for the True Cross*, Phoenix, 2000.

16. Jacobus de Voragine, *The Golden Legend*, c. 1260.

17. *Chronicle of Lantercost* (1272 – 1346)

18. See, for example, http://www.doncaster.gov.uk/
Leisure_and_Culture/Museums_and_Galleries/
Learning_and_Access_Zone/Romans_on_the_Don/
Barnsdale_Bar.asp

15th Degree

1. See, for example, http://www.britannia.com/
history/arthur/cross.html

2. See, for example, http://en.wikipedia.org/wiki/
Castel_del_Monte,_Apulia

3. See, for example http://www.charmingitaly.com/
castel-del-monte/

4. See, for example, http://www.facebook.com/pages/
Orval-Abbey/107625912600902

5. For a good explanation of this concept, see, http://
en.wikipedia.org/wiki/Davidic_line

6. The idea that the Sphinx was constructed around
BC 10,000 or before is covered well in Bauval,
Robert and Hancock, Graham, *Keepers of Genesis*,
Arrow, 1997.

7. One explanation of the eagle's association with
Scorpio can be found at, http://www.novia.
net/~aaronk/ast/scorpio.html

8. D. Davidson and H. Aldersmith, *The Great
Pyramid: Its Divine Message*, 1924.

1. Peacham, Henry, *Minerva Britanna, A Garden of Heroical Devices, Furnished, and Adorned with Emblems and Impresa's of Sundry Natures, Newly Devised, Moralized,* 1612.

2. An article discussing this scam can be found at, http://www.astrocat.exactpages.com/ye2003.html

3. See, R. N. Mantegna, S. V. Buldyrev, A. L. Goldberger, S. Havlin, C. K. Peng, M. Simons, and H. E. Stanley, Linguistic Features of Noncoding DNA Sequences, Phys. Rev. Lett. 73, 3169 (1994)

4. The Kirkwall Scroll is a manuscript of unknown origin that hangs on the west wall of the Lodge Kirkwall Kilwinning, No. 38, in Orkney. It is said to be the most important Masonic manuscript known to the Order. It consists of a centre strip which contains around one hundred Masonic symbols, most of which relate to the quest to regain Paradise, and two outer strips containing maps. The inscriptions on the scroll are written in code and correspond to the secrets of the degree of Master of the Ninth Arch or The Royal Arch of Enoch. The high alter depicted on the scroll holds an inscription that reads: "I AM hath sent me unto you. I AM THAT I AM. I am the Rose of Sharon and the Lily of the Valley. I AM that I AM or I WILL BE that I WILL BE.

Illustration Acknowledgements

While every effort has been made to ensure that permissions are granted, if there are any errors or oversights regarding copyright material, we apologise and will make suitable acknowledgment in any future addition.

The publishers would like to thank, where appropriate, the following individuals and institutions for permission to reproduce copyright material:

1st Degree Figures

1. Private Collection.

2. Private Collection. Many examples of this image exist, such as in a printed book issued in 1788, published by Joh. Ad. Eckhardt, Book-Printer to H.M. the King of Denmark, entitled, *The Teachings of the Rosicrucians of the 16th and 17th Centuries or A Simple ABC Booklet For Young Students Practising Daily in the School of the Holy Ghost Made clear to the eyes by pictorial figures For the Exercises of the New Year In the Natural and Theological Light by a Brother of the Fraternity of the Rose Cross Christi P.F. For the first time made public and with several figures of similar content added by P.S. Altona.* Also in the

Altona Manuscript, published in 1785, under the title *Geheime Figuren der Rosenkreuzer*, or *Secret Symbols of the Rosicrucians*.

3. Private Collection.

4. Private Collection.

5. Private Collection.

6. Private Collection.

7. Private Collection.

8. Private Collection.

2nd Degree Figures

9. Image sent to author by Thomas Anderson, Adept of the 9th Temple Degree. It must be assumed that this is a photocopy of the introduction that appears in an original version of *New Atlantis* published by Andrew Hebb, London, At the Bell in St. Paul's churchyard, c.1627.

10. Private Collection. Other versions of the seal can be found in the Bodleian Library Michael MS. 276. An equivalent figure also appears in a Latin version, Bodleian Library, Aubrey MS. 24, dated to 1674.

3rd Degree Figures

7. Private Collection.

6. Private Collection.

11. Private Collection. A good example of the cylinder seal depicting Tammuz and Gishzida can also be found in Zecharia Sitchin, *The 12th Planet*, Avon Books, 1978, p, 166.

12. Private Collection. A good example can also be found in *Le Triomphe Hermetique*, from *Collectanea chymica* 1693 and *Le Triomphe Hermetique* Limojon de Saint-Didier 8°, Amsterdam, 1689.

13. Private Collection. An example of the cup can be found published as fig. 368c in William Hayes Ward, *The Seal cylinders of Western Asia*, Washington, 1910.

14. Private Collection. A comparable image can be found in Wallis Budge, *Gods of the Egyptians*, Vol.1, 1908. Plate entitled, *Thoth, the scribe of the Gods*.

15. Image sent by source from British Museum, *Department of the Middle East*.

16. Private Collection. A comparable image can be found in *Mercurius Trismegistus*, found in Francofurti: Sumptibus Ludovicj Bourgeat, *Historia deorum fatidicorum*, 1680, plate opposite p. 37.

17. Image sent to author by Thomas Anderson, Adept of the 9th Temple Degree. It must be assumed that this is a photocopy of the introduction that

appears in an original version of *New Atlantis* published by Andrew Hebb, London, At the Bell in St. Paul's churchyard, c.1627.

18.   Private Collection.

19.   Private Collection.

5th Degree Figures

20.   Having revisited the library recently to acquire the exact reference to the 16th century *Camdeni Britannia* volume, the librarian was unable to locate it. But a reference to the same pyramid forms can be found at http://www.philological.bham.ac.uk/cambrit/yorkslat.html

21.   Private Collection.

22.   Private Collection.

23.   Private Collection.

24.   Private Collection.

6th Degree Figures

25.   With thanks to The Whitworth Art Gallery, Manchester. This image also appears in Bernard E. Jones, *Freemasons' Guide and Compendium*, George G. Harrap & Company LTD, 1950, Plate 1.

26.   Private Library. A comparable image can also be found in E. A. Wallis Budge, *The Book of the Cave*

of Treasures, Abraham and the city of Ur, London, The Religious Tract Society, plate XI, no.2 p. 257, 1927.

27. Private Library. A comparable image can be found in a GUIDE-BOOK to the IRAQ MUSEUM, Illustration 38, 1973.

28. Private Collection.

29. Private Collection.

30. Private Collection. A comparable image can be found in, *First Degree*, International Co-Freemasonry (1925 Working Revised), pp. 88-89.

31. Private Collection. This image can be found in several Rosicrucian works, but one of the most compelling uses exists in Michael Maier, *Atalanta Fugiens, hoc est, Emblemata Nova de Secretis Naturae Chymica*, Oppenheim: Johann Theodori de Bry, emblem 21, 1617.

7th Degree Figures

32. Private Collection. The original, more detailed etching by Blake can be found at, http://www.themorgan.org/collections/works/blake/work.asp?id=onDisplay&page=1

33. Private Collection. The original, more detailed etching by Blake can be found at, http://www.blakearchive.org/exist/blake/archive/object.xq?objectid=jerusalem.e.illbk.100&java=yes

34. With thanks to Tate,/Digital Image © Tate, London 2011.

8th Degree Figures

35. Private Collection.

36. Private Collection.

37. Private Collection.

38. Private Collection.

39. Private Collection.

40. Halfpenny. J, Gothic Ornaments in the Cathedral Church of York, Plate located to the back of the book, 1795. Proofs for the first addition can be found in York Local History Library.

11. Private Collection. A good example of the cylinder seal depicting Tammuz and Gishzida can also be found in Zecharia Sitchin, *The 12th Planet*, Avon Books, 1978, p, 166.

41. Private Collection.

9th Degree Figures

1. Private Collection.

42. The image (centre) appears in, C. Larkin, *The Book of Revelation: A Study of the Last Prophetic Book of the Bible*, 1919, p. 89. The image (right) Private Collection is in the style of *Our*

Lady of Guadalupe (Spanish: *Nuestra Señora de Guadalupe*), but it is most likely related to events in Revelation. The image (left) Private Collection.

43. As 1 and 42.

44. Private Collection.

45. Private Collection.

46. Private Collection.

47. Private Collection.

48. Private Collection.

49. Private Collection.

50. Private Collection.

10th Degree Figures

51. Private Collection.

52. Private Collection.

53. Private Collection.

54. Many examples of this image exist, such as in a printed book issued in 1788, published by Joh. Ad. Eckhardt, Book-Printer to H.M. the King of Denmark, entitled, *The Teachings of the Rosicrucians of the 16th and 17th Centuries or A Simple ABC Booklet For Young Students Practising Daily in the School of the Holy Ghost Made clear to the eyes by pictorial figures For the Exercises of the New Year In the Natural and*

Theological Light by a Brother of the Fraternity of the Rose Cross Christi P.F. For the first time made public and with several figures of similar content added by P.S. Altona. Also in the *Altona Manuscript*, published in 1785, under the title *Geheime Figuren der Rosenkreuzer*, or *Secret Symbols of the Rosicrucians.*

55. Private Collection. From Robert Fludd's title page for *Utriusque cosmi historia*, Oppenheim, 1617.

31. Private Collection. This image can be found in several Rosicrucian works, but one of the most compelling uses exists in Michael Maier, Atalanta Fugiens, hoc est, Emblemata Nova de Secretis Naturae Chymica, Oppenheim: Johann Theodori de Bry, emblem 21, 1617.

56. Private Collection.

57. Private Collection.

11th Degree Figures

58. Private Collection.

59. Private Collection.

60. Private Collection.

61. Private Collection.

62. Private Collection.

63. Private Collection.